THE **POCKET IDIOT'S GUIDE** TO

Home Inspections

by Bobbi Dempsey and Mike Kuhn

ALPHA

A member of Penguin Group (USA) Inc.

International Standard Book Number: 1-59257-216-2
Library of Congress Catalog Card Number: 2004100496

06   05   04   8   7   6   5   4   3   2   1

Interpretation of the printing code: The rightmost number of the first series of numbers is the year of the book's printing; the rightmost number of the second series of numbers is the number of the book's printing. For example, a printing code of 04-1 shows that the first printing occurred in 2004.

Printed in the United States of America

Contents

Introduction

Just as people wander around a car lot, occasionally kicking a tire without really knowing why, many homeowners have no idea how to evaluate their home.

To a certain extent, that's okay. After all, you're not supposed to be an expert—that's the home inspector's job. But you should have a basic understanding of your home's systems and components. And by brushing up on your "home smarts" prior to an inspection, you'll be better able to ask questions and to understand exactly what the inspector is talking about.

You'll also learn why a home inspector may barely bat an eyelash at that ugly—yet purely cosmetic—defect in your home, while he or she becomes deeply concerned over something structural that you never even noticed.

The most important words of wisdom in the book boil down to two main things: the potential problems related to each of your home's systems, and the bottom line of what it'll cost you to fix.

Extras

In addition, you'll find some extra little tips and tidbits:

Nuts and Bolts _____

Quick little tips and snippets of info.

 House Keys _____

Definitions of important terms.

 Home Alarms _____

Warnings and important information to be aware of.

 **Something to Dwell On** _____

Interesting facts and stuff you probably didn't know.

Acknowledgments

Bobbi Dempsey would like to thank—first and foremost—her co-author Mike, because without his tireless advice and guidance, you wouldn't be reading this book right now. And three people she inexcusably neglected to thank in a previous book—her brothers Joe and Bill, and her good friend Lisa Beamer. Also, Alyson O'Mahoney of Robin Leedy & Associates and Jessica Faust of

BookEnds. And, of course, Jack, John, Nick, and Brandon can never go unmentioned.

From Mike Kuhn: After 17 years as a HouseMaster franchisee, and home inspector, I feel fortunate to be able to share what I have learned with all the future homebuyers and owners alike. However, this would not be possible without the help of my wife, Kathleen, who also shares a passion for this business and now serves as president and CEO of HouseMaster. Also, thanks to Ken Austin, chairman of HouseMaster, who through the years has provided the guidance and opportunity to grow my business into the multiple franchise operation it is today. And, lastly, thanks to the staff at the National Institute of Building Inspectors (NIBI), Joe Cummins, John Hendricks, and Joe Tangradi, who have provided so much technical information and support required to succeed in this business. Thank you to all.

Trademarks

Home Inspections 101

In This Chapter

- What is a home inspection?
- Lots of people need home inspections
- How to prepare

Admit it, the last time you went house-hunting, you probably checked out the local school district, investigated property taxes, and perhaps even did some discreet snooping on your potential new neighbors. But did you get down on your hands and knees searching for cracks in the foundation? Haul out the ladder and investigate roof flashings? More than likely, you skipped those messy jobs and were instead busy debating whether the current carpeting would clash with your furniture. Plus, let's face it, when you've already fallen in love with the walk-in closets and the window seat, can you really be objective about any structural problems lurking behind the bay windows in the house you're eyeing up?

And, if you're considering selling a property, you're even less likely to check out your home's nooks and crannies for possible problems. "What I don't know won't hurt me," you may think …

But what you don't know *can* hurt you—sometimes literally, in the case of serious safety hazards and maintenance problems in the home. It can also be painful financially, because if a buyer feels you have hidden flaws or maintenance problems with their home, they can demand you do the repairs or reimburse them for the cost.

How Do You Know What to Look For?

The average homeowner doesn't know what to look for—which is why you need a thorough *home inspection* done by a qualified inspector. The home inspector's job is to examine the overall condition of a home and its systems and components including electrical, plumbing, and mechanical items, such as the furnace and water heater.

The home inspector thoroughly examines all of your home's major parts, paying particular attention to any safety hazards. After identifying any problem areas, the home inspector may recommend *further evaluation*.

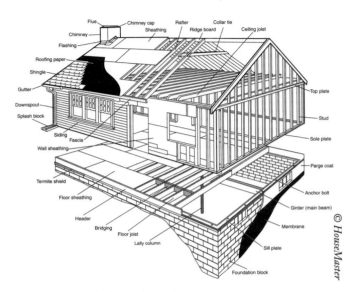

An example of a home schematic.

House Keys

A **home inspection** is a process by which an inspector visually examines the readily accessible systems and components of a home, and evaluates those components according to established standards. **Further evaluation** means examination and analysis by a qualified professional or service technician beyond that provided by the home inspection. For example, if a home inspector suspects a problem with your wiring, he or she will likely recommend further evaluation by a qualified electrician.

A home inspector should not, however, make specific recommendations on how to make repairs or fix things. It would also be unethical for a home inspector to recommend a specific electrician or other specialist.

A home inspection is not the same as a code inspection. Code-enforcement officers work for municipalities, and concentrate strictly on enforcing the local codes. A code-enforcement officer determines how your home and property stacks up against codes and regulations, while a home inspector makes his or her evaluation based on accepted standards of practice—minimum, uniform standards for home inspections, established by organizations such as the National Institute of Building Inspectors (NIBI), American Society of Home Inspectors (ASHI), or industry publications.

For example, a code, enforcement officer might worry about your pool being a little too close to your property line, if it presents a possible violation of local ordinances. That wouldn't be a big concern to a home inspector, though, unless it somehow presented a major safety hazard. Also, in many areas, a home built prior to the existence of a specific code may be "grandfathered" if it does not meet the standards of that code. A home inspector evaluates a home according to current safety standards and practices.

When the inspection is completed, you will receive an inspection report. Some firms, such as co-author Mike's company, HouseMaster, provide "instant" reports immediately after the inspection. Other companies send their reports by mail or fax.

Can't I Do It Myself?

Even if you happen to have some home maintenance or construction experience, it's pretty unlikely that you'd be familiar with all the aspects of home construction. A good home inspector has probably done hundreds of inspections, and is knowledgeable about all of a home's components and systems and can easily spot potential problem areas.

Also, it's very tough to be totally objective about a home you're hoping to buy or sell. An inspector can evaluate the home with an unbiased eye.

What Will It Cost?

A home inspection for a typical one-family house usually costs between $300 and $500. However, prices can vary geographically, and can also differ depending on the home's size, age, and other specific features. You will also pay more if you want "extra" inspection services, such as those involving pools, spas, landscaping, etc. Should an inspection reveal problem areas that you later get repaired, some companies will perform a re-inspection at a lower fee.

Don't choose a home inspector based on price alone, though. You often do get what you pay for, and the lowest-priced inspector may also be the least qualified. And an unqualified or inexperienced home inspector won't be a good bargain in the long run.

Naturally, inspection services that offer "extras" such as radon inspections or septic system evaluations as part of their routine inspection will probably charge somewhat more than companies that don't. So if you're doing price comparisons, be sure to find out exactly which services each company's inspection includes.

Something to Dwell On _____

The average American family spends about a third of their monthly income on housing. That's a big investment—and a good reason to give your home an occasional check-up.

Buyers Beware

Really, anyone who lives in a house can benefit from a home inspection. After all, you probably get your car inspected once a year, though you most likely spend a lot more time in your house.

There are specific groups of people who can particularly benefit from a home inspection. The majority of people who order home inspections are homebuyers, followed by sellers. Landlords also occasionally seek home inspections.

Okay, so you've got your eye on that cute little Cape Cod with the tree house and in-ground pool. You're not exactly objective at this point—after all, you're already scouting out the perfect place for that vegetable garden you've always wanted. Wouldn't you also want to know the true condition of what you may invest your life savings in? Take off those rose-colored glasses—or let the home inspector serve as the objective judge.

Naturally, the seller may not be too eager to point out the little details about the home's structural conditions or maintenance issues. And the realtor? Uh, does the word "commission" ring a bell?

Something to Dwell On

In a survey of real-estate agents conducted by the American Society of Home Inspectors, 92 percent of respondents said they always recommend that buyers get a home inspection, while another 7 percent said they often make this recommendation.

A home inspector can give an unbiased, objective evaluation of the home's condition. The home inspector's job is not to try and talk you out of buying the home, or even to give you ammunition for getting the sellers to lower their price. A home inspector simply wants to help you make an informed decision, and avoid any unpleasant (and potentially expensive) surprises down the road.

The home inspector may even bring some good news—perhaps the home's actually in even better shape than you thought. Get ready to dive into that pool!

Timing Is Everything

When should a prospective homebuyer order an inspection? Some buyers may consider having a home inspection performed prior to making an offer on a home. This may sound like good advice, saving time by eliminating the possibility of a deal falling through, but it may actually be counterproductive. For example, buyers can make lowball offers based upon pre-contract inspections, thus turning off sellers.

You should, however, order a home inspection soon after your purchase offer has been accepted and you've signed an *agreement of sale*. Many real-estate contracts allow a limited number of days to complete a home inspection (and then to request repairs, or cancel the contract if needed).

House Keys

An **agreement of sale** is a contract between the buyer and seller involving the purchase of a home. These contracts generally specify certain conditions—possibly including negative findings in a home inspection—that would render the agreement void.

Especially for Home Sellers

Sure it may seem counter-intuitive—or just plain dumb—to blab every little detail about your home's condition (especially the not-so-great parts) to prospective buyers. But, in fact, sellers can actually use home inspections to their advantage in several ways.

If you've recently replaced one or more major systems in your home, if your home was well maintained (and is perhaps in better shape than most houses of the same age), or if the home has any structural features that are particularly impressive—well, this is all something you want to promote to potential buyers. And a home-inspection report is the perfect way to do it in writing (without looking like you're bragging about your incredible Mr. Fix-It skills).

For sellers, it's a good idea to get a home inspection as soon as you begin contemplating selling your home. This way, you'll know right away how the home fares, and will be well informed early in the process. Should the inspection reveal possible problems, you can decide whether to address them before listing the home.

Especially for Landlords and Renters

What if you're not in the market to buy or sell a home, but simply want to make a few bucks renting out a property? Well, you, too, can benefit from a home inspection.

Let's face it—we live in a lawsuit-happy society. Should your tenant happen to trip over his or her own two feet, he or she can surely find a lawyer who'll be happy to try and convince a court that your floor wasn't level, the carpeting was loose—or perhaps your house just has plain old "bad karma." An inspection report can help protect you by providing an official record of the property's condition.

Besides, just as sellers need to make their homes look good to buyers, landlords also need to make their properties look enticing enough to catch renters' eyes. By offering prospective tenants written proof of the home's condition, you'll stand out from the pack.

If you're a renter and your landlord didn't order a home inspection, it may be to your advantage to get one on your own. True, it'll come out of your own pocket, but inspections are relatively inexpensive—especially when compared to paying a year's rent on a place that isn't in the greatest shape (a fact you may not discover until after you sign the lease).

Also, if you have renters' insurance (which is definitely a good idea), your agent may require an inspection—or give you a discount if you get one.

Getting Ready for the Inspection

Make sure the inspector can easily access and evaluate the entire property, especially all the home's *systems* and *components*.

House Keys _____

A **system** is a combination of interacting or interdependent components, assembled to carry out one or more functions. Examples include the heating system and the structural system. A **component** is a smaller part of that system. For example, the foundation is a component of the structural system.

Remove furniture, boxes, or other items that might obstruct the inspector's view of an important system or component. The inspector will need to enter the basement and attic, so be sure those entranceways are clear.

Try to schedule the inspection for a time when the kids will be at school or otherwise occupied, so as not to distract you or the inspector. If your pets tend to be nervous or aggressive around strangers—especially strangers who will be poking around their territory—it might be a good idea to have someone else watch Fido while the inspection is going on.

Check (and if necessary, replace) the bulbs in all interior and exterior light fixtures. The inspector will have no way of knowing whether the lights work if the bulbs are dead.

Make sure you have keys readily available for any areas that may be locked at the time of the inspection. Bottom line: Make sure everything a home inspector needs to see is readily accessible.

If the home is vacant, confirm that the seller will have all utilities on during the home inspection. Failure to do so may require a second trip to the home when the utilities are on, and you will incur additional fees. To properly evaluate a home, a professional inspector must be able to operate the systems, thus requiring the utilities to be on.

The Least You Need to Know

- A home inspection isn't a do-it-yourself project, even if you have some construction experience.

- A typical home inspection costs between $300 and $500, but prices can vary greatly.

- Home inspections can benefit buyers, sellers, landlords, and renters.

- An inspector can't evaluate what he or she can't see, so be sure all parts of the property are visible and accessible.

Starting at the Top: The Roof

In This Chapter

- Out of sight, not out of mind
- Flashings, fiberglass, and other important stuff
- Keep repair bills from going through the roof

Many people barely give their roof a second thought. It's at the tip-top of your home, but may be far down on your priority list. You can't really see it, so it's easy to neglect it. But the roof is a vital part of your home—a shield to protect the rest of the home. Your roof keeps undesirable stuff like rain, snow, and other elements from getting in, while keeping valuable heat and energy from getting out. So just how good is the roof over *your* head?

Important Roofing Terms

Here are a few important basic roofing terms that will be helpful to you in understanding roof concerns:

- Eaves: The horizontal, lower edge of a sloped roof.
- Rise: The vertical distance from the eaves line to the ridge.
- Run: The horizontal distance from the eaves to a point directly under the ridge. Equals one half the span.
- Span: The horizontal distance from eaves to eaves.
- Slope: The degree of roof-incline expressed as the ratio of the rise to the run.
- Pitch: The degree of roof-incline expressed as the ratio of the rise to the span.
- Shingles: Cut to a specific size and smooth-finished. Shakes are irregular and rough-textured.

Understanding Slope

Slope and pitch are both terms to indicate the incline of a sloping roof. Although the terms are often interchanged, they actually mean two different things. For simplicity's sake, we will address slope, as it is generally the method of determining the proper roof material. Picture a right triangle.

The height of the triangle in the rise, the length of the base is the run, and the line between the top of the rise to the end of the run is the slope.

There are different materials for different slopes. For example, steep roofs will be suitable for all type of shingles: slate, wood, tile, etc. Low-slope roofs should have rolled roofing material, and flat roofs should have rolled roofing, membrane, or built-up roofing materials.

Flat and low-slope roofs are more prone to leaks than the steeper varieties, so you need to keep an eye on them. And when leaks do occur, it's tougher to spot and fix them on a flat or low-slope roof. It can also sometimes be tricky to pinpoint the exact source of a leak because water can enter the roof from one side, migrate under built-up roof layers, and enter the house from another side. Since flat and low-slope roofs tend to be less "visible" than their steeper counterparts, often the flatter varieties tend to be neglected.

Common Problems, by Roof Type

Specific roof types have distinct "red flags" that are sure signs of problems.

Tile: Watch for cracked and broken tiles, missing or loose tiles, fastener corrosion, and loose tiles that have been set in mortar. Discoloration, scaling, and other surface damage indicate possible water-absorption problems, which may lead to entire roof failure in areas with freeze/thaw cycles.

Slate roofs: Concerns will include cracked and broken slates, loose slates, flaking, scaling, and fastener corrosion.

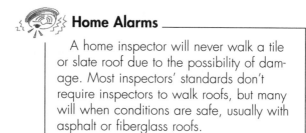

Home Alarms

A home inspector will never walk a tile or slate roof due to the possibility of damage. Most inspectors' standards don't require inspectors to walk roofs, but many will when conditions are safe, usually with asphalt or fiberglass roofs.

Wood: Watch out for loose and missing shingles, cracking, and splitting. Cracking and splitting indicates that the roof is drying out, which will only worsen as the roof ages. Curling and lifting are signs of a lower-quality product in addition to drying out. Excessive curling offers no protection against wind-driven rain and is as bad as missing shingles. Mildew and decay are also signs of trouble. Moss buildup indicates ongoing presence of high moisture. If there is moisture, there is wood decay. Excessive decay will obviously lead to roof failure. In home inspection terms, "failure" means not functioning as intended, and requiring repair or replacement.

Asphalt/fiberglass shingle: Curling shingle tabs, granule loss, cracking or splitting, wear between the tabs (keyways).

Flat: Cracking or alligatoring, lifted seams, physical damage, water between the membranes, etc.

> ### Something to Dwell On _____
>
> About 1 in 10 residential roofs is covered with wood—mainly red cedar, which has a natural resistance to decay. Wood roofing comes in the form of shingles or the more expensive shakes. Both are available in a range of grades, based on quality.

The Fix

If you have some handyman skills, you might be able to tackle an asphalt roofing project yourself. Tile and slate roof products, on the other hand, can be challenging to install (and since these are among the most expensive roofing materials, you don't want to take the chance of wasting supplies).

If a small number of shingles are damaged or missing, simply repairing that small section is probably the most cost-effective way to go. For a 100-square-foot section, figure at least $100 for asphalt shingles and $250 or more for cedar shingles. However, if a large portion of the roof is affected, you should probably replace the entire roof.

When the surface of a flat roof is worn or damaged, it's generally best to remove the roofing material all the way down to solid decking. This is really the only way to visibly inspect the condition of the roof framing.

Financial Damages

Costs are rough estimates for an average-size home (around 1500 square feet) and standard materials. Costs will increase if you have a larger home or want high-end materials.

Supplies only:

- 30-year asphalt shingles: $1000
- 16-inch cedar shingles: $2000
- 24-inch cedar shakes: $3000

Hiring a professional:

- Installing new asphalt shingles over existing layer: $1500 and up
- Removing several layers of shingles and replacing with plywood and shingles: $4000
- Removing several layers of shingles and replacing with polymembrane flat roofing: $5000–$7500

Roof Age

Estimating a roof's age is not as difficult as many people believe. First, consider the age of the house. A 15-year-old house typically still has its original roof. If the roof is asphalt/fiberglass, the normal life expectancy of this roof would be 20 to 25 years

for a good-quality shingle, and more or less as
quality goes up or down. In this example you could
expect, under normal conditions, another 5 or 10
years of life on the roof. On the other hand, if you
have a 28-year-old house with its original roof, the
roof would already be several years beyond normal
life expectancy and most likely would need to be
replaced soon.

 Home Alarms

> Because two layers of shingles are
> allowed in most areas, on a 38-year-old
> house you may find "multiple layers." This
> means that in approximately two years a
> complete "tear-off" will be required. This
> requires stripping off all roofing material
> down to wood underlayment/sheathing
> and putting a roof on from scratch. This
> will add significantly to the cost of re-
> roofing.

Roof Ventilation

It's important to give attics "breathing room" as in
the following figure. Improper or inadequate ventilation can lead to overheating and moisture buildup. This can cause stifling indoor temperatures,
especially in warmer months. It can also accelerate
wear and tear on the roofing materials. The moisture buildup can cause mold, mildew, and fungus to
form and spread. Excessive heat and moisture can

also eventually lead to major concerns such as roof or sheathing failure.

An attic ventilator.

Even in cold weather, moisture buildup can be a problem, creating damaging condensation on cold roof sheathing.

Keep an eye out for mold or mildew or other ugly growths on interior or exterior areas of attic ceilings, walls, or the roof. Also, watch out for premature deterioration of the roof shingles on the exterior.

The Fix

Always keep attic vents open or unblocked in summer and winter, year-round. A "cold attic" is desirable. Vent openings should not be sealed or obstructed by insulation.

Soffit vents, which can be effective "passive" ventilation methods, should be located under the roof sections that overhang the exterior walls of the house. They will enable air to flow upward on the underside of the roof sheathing and exit through a ridge vent. A continuous ridge vent is preferred, as it is a weather-protected opening running the length of the roof at its peak. Electric exhaust fans are typically thermostatically controlled and will only operate at pre-set temperature settings.

House Keys _____

A **soffit** is the finished underside of the eaves.

Financial Damages

Ventilation options range from no-cost passive ventilation to bigger-ticket items such as electric exhaust fans, which can cost $100 and up. However, these are wise investments, compared to the price of roof repairs and when you factor in potential energy savings.

Flashing

Surprisingly, most roof leaks are caused, not by worn roofing materials, but by missing or defective *flashings*. A flashing is a barrier, usually aluminum, copper, galvanized steel, or an asphalt-based membrane, or roll roofing that seals the joint(s) when a roof plane is interrupted—such as by skylights, vent pipes, and chimneys—or altered by valleys or gables. The flashing is designed to divert water away from the joint to prevent interior water penetration.

House Keys

A **flashing** is a barrier that seals the joint(s) when a section of roof is interrupted or altered.

Flashing comes in a wide variety of types and styles, with the specific choice often dictated by the roof style.

No matter what the style, all flashings need constant monitoring and occasional maintenance for problems due to improper installation or simple normal aging. Watch for flashings that have dried out, ripped, or are otherwise ineffective at providing a watertight seal. See the photo that follows for an example of flashing that has deteriorated.

Deteriorated flashing is a leak waiting to happen.

The Fix

Flashings should be repaired or replaced immediately upon any signs of damage or leaks. Small areas of loose, bent, corroded, or otherwise damaged flashing can usually be reinstalled or permanently patched with similar material. More serious damage or a problem involving a larger section of flashing generally requires total replacement.

Home Alarms

> Re-roofing typically does not include new flashings. The existing/original flashings are left in place, or are re-used. A new roof is no guarantee against a flashing leak.

Financial Damages

Flashings are relatively easy and inexpensive to repair or replace. The key is to catch problems early, before they lead to costly water damage. Repairing or replacing a small portion of flashing will usually cost $150 and up. Totally replacing the flashing on an average home will cost between $400 and $800.

Fiberglass Roofing

For many years, asphalt was king when it came to roofing shingles. But these days, fiberglass asphalt materials—most commonly used in the form of shingles—are the most common residential roof product.

New fiberglass materials are much stronger and more durable than earlier versions. There are some all-fiberglass roof applications that can actually be walked on and support furniture. The versatility of fiberglass roofing materials—it's available in a wide variety of colors and styles—makes it very popular and a good choice for just about any style of home.

Fiberglass asphalt shingles are comparable in price to traditional asphalt products and, because of their durability, may be a more cost-effective choice.

All roofs are subject to cracking as they age, but cracking in a relatively new roof in a distinct pattern is often the first sign of a defective fiberglass roof.

 Nuts and Bolts

> Fiberglass asphalt shingles are covered by a standard called ASTM D-3462, which requires products to pass tear-strength and nail-withdrawal tests. When buying fiberglass shingles, be sure to look for the ASTM D-3462 certification on the label.

Skylights

Skylights—which can be used to brighten dark rooms, hallways, and even porches—are an extremely popular home accent these days, but are also a common "hot spot" for problems—mainly due to improper installation.

Potential Problem

With skylights, it's all about the installation. If the skylight wasn't properly installed, you'll have a problem. Usually a wet problem.

The main problem with skylights is the possibility of leaks. Keep an eye out for any signs of water penetration, because a leak will only grow worse—and fast. In other words, take action as soon as you spot the first drop of water!

In addition to the obvious signs of water (as in, dripping), watch for any buckling or warping of the ceiling area surrounding the skylight.

Financial Damages

A faulty or improperly installed skylight is often tough to repair, so you'll usually need to completely replace the entire skylight. Don't procrastinate in addressing a skylight problem, or you may find yourself with some additional expenses as a result of water damage.

If you have some basic handyman skills and aren't nervous about climbing around on the roof, you can probably install a self-flashing skylight yourself. If your roof is very steep, the skylight is very large, or you're nervous about possibly damaging your tile or other expensive roofing materials, then hire a professional.

Skylight (materials only): $250 and up

Skylight (materials and professional installation): $500 and up

The Least You Need to Know

- You can save big bucks by fixing your own roof, but know when to call in a professional.

- Take the slope of your roof into consideration when choosing roofing materials.

- Inexpensive tactics, such as passive ventilation, can be a real money-saver in preventing roof damage.

- Fiberglass is a durable, cost-effective roofing option.

- Most roof leaks are caused by missing or defective flashings.

- Skylights are a common source of leaks, and improper installation is often to blame.

Plumbing: Will Your Money Go Down the Drain?

In This Chapter

- Types of pipe and why it matters
- A little noise can mean big trouble
- Common water-heater problems

Plumbing is one of the most important systems in the house. And it often seems like plumbing problems arise at the worst possible times—like when you've just lathered up your hair in the shower and suddenly you're jolted by icy cold water. Components of the plumbing system are also among the most heavily used parts of your house.

Unfortunately, plumbing problems can often involve big repair bills, so it's crucial to keep a close eye on your plumbing system (see the figure that follows for information on a typical plumbing system) and catch problems while they're still manageable and relatively inexpensive to fix.

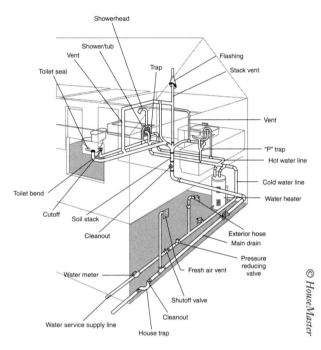

Overview of a typical residential plumbing system.

Main Water Source

You should know whether your water source is from a municipal supply or a well. In some instances there may be a community well, which services multiple private residences, and the owners all pay for the upkeep and testing.

Inspectors start their evaluation of the plumbing system where the water line enters the house.

There will usually be a meter here (the main shut-off) or a well storage tank and equipment.

 Nuts and Bolts

> Water flow will usually be lower from wells than on municipal systems. Typical pressure ranges will be 40-60 psi for a well and 60-80 psi for municipal. If your pressure is too high, this can damage the fixtures. In some cases, a home may be equipped with a pressure-reduction valve to reduce high pressure from the street.

Water-Supply Lines and Piping

Note the type and condition of water distribution pipes; these pipes are typically constructed of copper, brass, or galvanized steel. Copper is generally seen as the most desirable choice.

Galvanized pipes tend to corrode on the inside, sort of like a clogged artery. The condition is not visible by looking at the pipe, but telltale signs include reduced water flow when flushing a toilet. Problems will also develop when newer copper pipes are added to older galvanized pipes; this can cause a galvanic reaction, resulting in corrosion of the pipes where they're joined together, resulting in leakage. Galvanized pipes are no longer used for water-supply piping in homes. If a house does still have galvanized pipes, chances are good that it will soon need a completely new piping system, probably costing a minimum of $3,000.

Home Alarms

A home inspector is not required to check your washing machine hookups, wells, or lawn sprinklers. Some inspectors will do these added procedures for an extra fee, though. Ask around to find out what is customary in your area.

Waste Lines

Waste lines are also known as drain waste and vent pipes. Important things to note are the types of pipe, along with proper venting and the pitch of the pipe. Inadequately pitched pipes will lead to poor drainage clogging and drain back-up. Waste lines will typically have removable caps to allow for snaking clogged plumbing lines.

Check exposed waste pipes, which are bigger than water pipes and are usually made of copper, cast iron, or plastic. Look for signs of leakage, such as rust, stains, or foul odors.

Proper venting is required for the removal of dangerous gases and odors from the sewer lines. Sump pump discharge into drains is typically not allowed, as the municipal treatment facility will be overburdened by treating rain water. More importantly, excessive discharge into a private system such as a septic system will lead to its premature failure. This is also true when leaky faucets, drains, etc., overload a septic system.

Noisy Water Pipes

You know what we're talking about. The banging, clanging noisy pipes. Especially common in older homes, this is a problem many people simply learn to live with. But you should pay attention to those noisy pipes, as they're sending you a loud and clear signal that plumbing problems may be in your future.

Noisy pipes are often caused by "water hammer." What the heck is a water hammer, you ask? Well, water hammer is basically the buildup of pressure in the water lines. It can be caused by several factors, including inadequately sized supply pipes and excessive water pressure. If you have banging, noisy pipes—especially if the noise occurs right after you turn your water faucet on or off—then you most likely have a water hammer problem. Sure, it's annoying, but that's the least of your worries. Water hammer can cause pipes to rupture and leak.

There are a few things you can do to lessen or eliminate water hammer:

- Use low-flow fixtures. Restricting water velocity helps reduce water hammer. This is the easiest and cheapest solution: A low-flow showerhead costs less than $20 and is easy to install.

- Install a pressure regulator. This lessens water hammer, costs around $20 (and up), but should really be installed by a professional.

- Have a professional install a water hammer arrester. This is the most effective solution. Prices range from $20 to $120, but probably not something you'd want to do yourself.

Fixtures and Drains

Watch for leaky faucets and fixtures. Also look for drains that gurgle, empty slowly, or spout air. And keep an eye on the seal between the sink and the drain—this is another common source of leaks.

 Nuts and Bolts

> Gurgling drains may indicate improper venting of the drainage system. This may be a result of poor original work, hair clogs, or even a botched "do-it-yourself" job. Further evaluation is required.

Like most experienced home inspectors, co-author Mike has developed a kind of sixth sense for detecting plumbing problems. "You turn on 20 thousand faucets and flush 20 thousand toilets, you sort of get to know right away."

Water Heaters

There are three different types of water heaters: gas, electric, and oil. Check the capacity and installation date by reading the label affixed to the water heater.

Electric water heaters recover more slowly than gas heaters and must hold approximately 50 percent more to be equivalent. Oil-fired water heaters, with a typical 30-gallon capacity, are adequate for the average-size family. These units normally last longer than others, but require more maintenance.

 Home Alarms

Most people don't really give their water heaters much thought—at least, not until they suddenly find themselves taking cold showers. However, HouseMaster found a serious and potentially dangerous condition present in about one of every five homes it inspected. When the relief valve is damaged or improperly installed, pressure can build. If this continues, eventually the heater can explode. The part is cheap to replace, but the condition is something most homeowners can't spot. Fortunately, a home inspector can recognize this problem right away.

Age of tank, venting, and condition of burner and combustion chamber are all important factors in evaluating a water heater. Typical equivalent sizes are electric, 50-gallon; gas, 40-gallon; and oil, 30-gallon. Hot-tub, Jacuzzi, or whirlpool owners will have to pay the price of indulgence, as this will require a greater-size water heater. For example, a 40-gallon heater will require an upgrade to at least 75 gallons. It will also depend on obvious factors, such as its age compared to normal life expectancy, leakage, whether it uses combustion air, and if it is installed properly for its location.

The photo that follows shows an example of soot near the burner, which is a sign of a water heater problem.

© HouseMaster

Excessive soot can be a signal of water heater problems.

Hot-Water Coil

Water boilers used for heating a home may also have a domestic hot-water coil as part of the system. This is an on-demand system, as there is no storage capacity. Cold water enters the coil, which is immersed in the already hot water within the boiler. Heat exchange takes place; the water comes out hot at the other end.

There are several drawbacks to a system that uses a hot-water coil:

- Temperature. The boiler water is 180 degrees, way too hot for domestic purposes. The boiler should feature a mixing valve. This enables more cold water to mix with the hot water as it exits the coil.

- You must run your boiler year-round to produce hot water. This may not be the most economical set-up.

- Lack of storage capacity. Coils tend to scale up over time, making heat transfer more difficult and causing hot water to run out quickly. Low storage capacity makes this problem much more obvious.

Nuts and Bolts _____

When evaluating the plumbing, you should let the water run for 5 to 10 minutes in order to get a clearer picture of how long the hot water maintains its temperature.

Say So Long to Sediment

Gas and oil water heaters may also have sediment buildup on the bottom of the tank. This acts as insulation between the burners and the water. The heater/burners must work harder to heat the water. This creates stress on the fiberglass tank that may result in leaks. Listening to a tank while the burners are on, you may hear popping noises. This is a result of sediment. The little drain valve at the bottom of the tanks is to drain a little water once or twice a year, thus flushing out sediment and prolonging the life of the tank.

Lead Water Pipes

A home inspector may be able to advise you if a lead water-supply pipe serves the building. This is generally only found in older homes. If so, excessive amounts of lead may be leaching into the water system. This is a potential health hazard. It's impractical to treat all of the water entering the home, but you can at least treat the drinking water. The best solution would be replacement of the lead water-service pipe, but this could cost thousands of dollars.

Water Quality

A home inspector will not test your water quality. If you have concerns about contamination, chlorine, or other undesirable stuff in your water, you should consider having a qualified inspector conduct a water-quality test. Generally, this involves sending a sample of your water to a lab for analysis.

Water testing is almost exclusively performed on well water from private wells, not municipal water supplies. One exception may be lead-in-water tests, since the source of the lead may be from plumbing. The state or municipality may require other tests, The most basic test would be for chloroform— many mortgage lenders require this. However, if you choose to get a water test, ask what is being tested for and how much it costs. Prices vary significantly from lab to lab and for each test. Basically, "water testing" is not all-inclusive.

Common Problems: Plumbing

Some of the most common plumbing problems include:

- Leaks in waste or supply lines or at fixtures.
- Leaks in pipes and joints.
- Undersized piping. Some homes may have $1/2$-inch tubing when $3/4$-inch tubing is called for. Low water flow may result with smaller pipes.
- Water heater not working, or not heating water quickly enough.

The Fix

When it comes to plumbing, anything more challenging than a clogged toilet is usually not something the average homeowner is willing or able to tackle. Repairing a small portion of pipe or replacing a broken/leaking faucet (either of which should cost less than $100) may be within the abilities of a do-it-yourselfer, but bigger jobs such as replacing a water heater are best left to the professionals.

 Home Alarms _____

> You can prevent your money from going down the drain with a few simple tricks. Most people have their water heater's temperature set too high. Lower yours to around 115 degrees, and you can shave up to 10 percent off the cost of running the heater. Cover your heater in insulation or water heater blankets, and you can double that savings.

The Bottom Line on Plumbing Problems

How much of your money will go down the drain if you have plumbing problems?

Replacing sections of pipe: $300 to $500

New water heater: $300 to $900

Replacing entire piping system: $3,000 to $5,000

We'll look at specific concerns/issues related to the shower, tub, and toilet in Chapter 9.

The Least You Need to Know

- It's important to spot plumbing problems before they get bigger—and more expensive.
- Water hammer can cause major damage to your plumbing system.
- Draining sediment from your water heater can prolong its life.

Electricity

In This Chapter

- Grounding, bonding, and other details
- Overloading fuses can be dangerous
- How GFCIs can save your life

Electricity is perhaps one of the most important systems in your home. It's constantly in use—and if you have a family full of kids who love TV, video games, computers, and other gadgets, the electricity gets very heavy usage.

From a safety aspect, electrical problems can be among the most hazardous home-maintenance deficiencies you can have.

Electricity should not be taken casually. Errors and poor work can result in property damage and serious personal injury. Translation: If there's one system of the house that do-it-yourself types should probably shy away from, it's the electrical system.

Something to Dwell On

According to a study done by co-author Mike's company, HouseMaster, electrical problems were the most common deficiencies found in home inspections. Deficiencies were found in 48.6 percent of homes that were 30 years old and up, in 30.3 percents of homes 13 to 29 years old, and in 14.1 percent of homes 1 to 12 years old.

Here is a basic diagram of a typical electrical system.

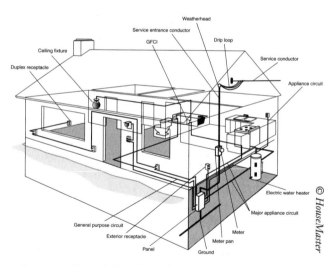

Overview of a typical residential electrical system.

Keep Three Things in Mind

All electrical work should comply with local and national electric code. While home inspectors typically do not perform code inspections, electrical systems are evaluated in terms of three important areas:

- Safety. For example, each major appliance should have its own circuit.

- Capacity. The system should meet the home's existing needs and have the capacity to accommodate room additions and new appliances.

- Convenience. There should be enough switches, lights, and outlets and they should be located so that occupants will not have to walk in the dark or use extension cords. By the way, the use of extension cords is the first red flag that the electrical system is not up to snuff.

 Nuts and Bolts

> While volts, amps, and ohms are better discussed in science class, the least you should know is that 100 amps is the minimum service recommended, and that 120/240 volts will be required to operate most major appliances such as a clothes dryer and central a/c unit.

Main Panel

The main panel is the central distribution point for the electrical circuits that run to lights, receptacles, and appliances throughout the house.

This is where you'll find the "main disconnect" or the fuse or circuit breaker that will disconnect the entire electrical system at one time. It is usually found at or within the main panel. The main disconnect must be readily accessible, and should never be located in a closet, behind locked doors, or where storage makes access difficult.

While examining the main panel, you'll note the amperage rating of your electrical service (this info should be clearly indicated). Although a 100-amp main will generally work fine for most homes, many builders now install 150-amp or 200-amp services just to be on the safe side.

Fuses

A fuse is an electrical overload protection device that will blow out if an overload occurs. Once the problem is fixed, the fuse will need to be replaced. Fuses are mainly found in older homes, as most modern homes use circuit breakers.

Fuses can be as safe and effective as circuit breakers if proper fuse sizes are used. The one big hazard of fuses is the ease of intentional or accidental overloading. If a glass fuse blows, there is nothing to prevent you from inserting an oversized fuse, as all fuses are all of similar sizes and appearance. Additionally, a homeowner may purposefully insert an oversized fuse in order to "correct" the problem, never addressing the reason why the fuse blew in the first place. Now a significant hazardous condition exists, as the wire carrying the increased load can overheat, causing a fire.

Fuse sizes will be listed right on the old fuse. The correct size should also be listed on the panel cover (it's a good idea to check the panel cover for the correct size, in case the old fuse was the wrong size). An experienced inspector can also check the wire gauge (size) to determine what size fuse should be used.

A 220 refers to volts and 30, 40, 50 refers to amps. Older homes only needed 30 to 50 amps and appliances used only 110 volts. As the electrical demands increased, so did the amount of power to the house increase, up to 100, 150, 200 amps. More powerful appliances such as electric stoves and dryers also required 220 volts. So a typical house has both 110/220 volts and is 110 to 200 amps.

 Home Alarms

> Fuses are cheap (a pack usually costs less than $5) and easy to replace, but be sure to use the correct size. Using an oversized fuse can cause overheating, which is a fire hazard.

Circuit Breakers

Circuit breakers are switches inside the electrical panel that will stop power to a certain area of the home in the event of a power overload. Once the problem is fixed, the circuit breaker can simply be switched back on.

Circuit breakers are very convenient in that they give a visual indication of having been tripped and can easily be reset. They are subject to deterioration, though, and should be tested regularly, especially as they age. An inspector will also check that breakers are properly labeled.

Red Flags

Keep an eye out for these signs of electrical problems:

- A low amp rating (such as less than 80 amps) could be a problem, as your system may not be able to handle your needs and may be prone to frequent overloads.
- If the main panel shows signs of corrosion, this may indicate a water or condensation problem.
- Circuit breakers and fuses should not have more than one electrical conductor attached to them.

Most of the problems could by rectified by a system upgrade (cost: $600 to $1200).

Electrical Service Upgrades

Many people think all their electrical problems will be solved by an electrical service upgrade, which typically includes a new service entry cable and panel box. What they fail to understand is that the original house wiring or branch circuit distribution is still in place. Having 1000 amps going into the house is no consolation to the homeowner who can't blow-dry his or her hair in the morning because the bathroom lacks any outlets.

The same is true for the person who can't plug in his or her new wide-screen TV for the big game because the family room only has one 15-amp outlet on the other side of the room. Distribution is just as important as service capacity. And adding new outlets and switches will certainly be as expensive if not more so than upgrading the service.

Sub-panels

Sub-panels are smaller electrical control panels that usually provide service to areas like the kitchen or entertainment room that may contain a lot of appliances or other devices requiring a lot of power. Sub-panels may be found in areas such as pools, spas, and additions. It's probably easier and less expensive to run one main line to a sub-panel and then run your branch circuits, rather than to run all branch circuits from a distant main panel.

Like the main panel, sub-panels also contain fuses or circuit breakers.

Service Entrance

The service entrance is the point where the electrical service enters the house. Basically, this is where any electrical problems now become your responsibility, rather than the power company's.

Evaluate the service entrance cables, insulation, *drip loop*, and conductors. Also, make sure that the *drop* and *weatherhead* are secure and in good condition.

> **House Keys**
>
> A **service drop** refers to the lines running from the pole to your house. A **drip loop** is a loop in the service conductor that minimizes the chance of water penetration. A **weatherhead** is a small cap attached to the building to keep the service entrance protected from the elements.

Fixtures and Outlets

A home inspector will evaluate your fixtures and outlets, and will test a representative number of them (generally, one per room). Keep an eye out for common problems such as loose receptacles or outlets that appear damaged or aren't functioning.

A common problem, especially in older homes, is too few outlets. This is generally just an inconvenience as opposed to a safety concern—unless it causes constant use of extension cords, which can be hazardous.

Junction Boxes

A junction box is a small box containing spliced or connected wiring and cables. Junction boxes must be closed (to protect wiring) and must be easily accessible.

A junction box is used when a branch circuit or wire is split off into a different direction or location. The spliced ends of the wire are put into a junction box to protect both the wire and the occupant.

Your inspector will likely check to ensure that junction boxes are closed and don't appear to be damaged or overloaded.

Ground Fault Circuit Interrupters (GFCI)

Ground fault circuit interrupters are outlets that provide extra protection against electrical shock in case of a short circuit. These outlets are usually found in kitchens, bathrooms, or outdoors and are easy to spot by the "test" and "reset" buttons in the center.

The following are GFCI requirements:

- 1970s to mid-1980s: exterior, bath, garage
- Late 1980s: add kitchen, basement, and boathouse
- 1990s: add wet bar, crawl space

> **Home Alarms** _____
>
> A GFCI can be a lifesaver because it senses very small differences in current between the hot and neutral wire in the outlet itself. Should you accidentally drop your blow dryer in the tub, the outlet itself senses this and will trip. On the other hand, a circuit breaker will not trip until its amp rating is exceeded (15–20 amp is typical). You will die at 1 amp.

Current inspection language will recommend at all these locations, regardless of the age of the house. Also included today are pools, spas, and whirlpools.

Wiring

Wiring is like the nerve system that distributes power throughout your house. Many wiring problems are caused by wiring that is too old, improperly used/installed, or that uses an outdated material.

Aluminum Wiring

Aluminum wiring was used in homes built beginning in the '60s. Builders initially thought it would be a good alternative to copper, but soon concerns arose about the tendency of aluminum wiring to overheat.

Nuts and Bolts

Wire thickness is the same as gauge; for example, #12 and #14 are typical branch circuit sizes.

Because aluminum wiring creates more resistance to electric current flow than copper, aluminum wiring must be one size larger than copper to carry the same load. If undersized, it will overheat. Aluminum also expands and contracts at a different rate than copper. As aluminum wiring expands and contracts with each use, the wire may distort and loosen. This may lead to sparking and igniting of nearby materials. Some signs of trouble include outlets that are warm to the touch, or flickering lights. Unfortunately, it's very difficult for homeowners to spot problems with aluminum wiring until it's too late—which is why you should probably consider doing a complete wiring overhaul.

Home inspectors generally recommend that an all-aluminum wiring system be checked by a licensed electrician, who'll ensure that proper remedial procedures have been taken so that the system meets accepted industry standards, which will vary from area to area.

Knob-and-Tube Wiring

"Knob-and-tube" wiring is an old type of wiring that is not grounded. As a result, ungrounded fixtures and outlets connected to this type of wiring could pose a safety hazard. Since this type of wiring hasn't been used in decades, though, any home containing knob-and-tube wiring is probably long overdue for an updated electrical system anyway.

 Home Alarms

> Insurance companies may deny your fire coverage if you have glass fuses or knob-and-tube wiring, as both types are considered a fire hazard for a variety of reasons.

Common Problems: Wiring

There are several common wiring-related concerns you should watch for, including:

- Exposed wires outside the junction boxes.
- Extension cords or other "temporary" measures being used for long-term wiring needs.
- Wiring that is lying on pipes (especially heat pipes).
- Wiring that is secured improperly.
- Spliced wiring that is not contained by a junction box or control panel.
- Wiring that is torn, deteriorated, or otherwise damaged.

Electric Meter

Generally, your electric meter is owned and maintained by the utility company, but you should still keep an eye on it for obvious problems or damage.

Smoke Detectors

A home inspector will note the presence of smoke detectors. He or she will not, however, check alarm systems. If that is something you'd like evaluated, look into getting a specialized inspection that focuses on alarm and security systems.

The Bottom Line on Electrical Repairs

The cost of electrical repairs and upgrades can be shocking, but don't be tempted to save a few bucks by trying to do it yourself unless you're extremely confident in your electrical skills. These jobs should generally be left to a professional:

- Adding/replacing electrical outlets and fixtures: $150 and up, each
- Replacing traditional outlet with GFCI: $75
- Replacing (single) circuit breaker: $50
- Installing circuit-breaker panel: $500 to $800
- Adding 240-volt circuit: $300
- Electrical service upgrade (usually includes new service entry cable and panel box): $600 to $1,200

- Total New Wiring System: $3,000 and up (Contrary to what most people think, this does not necessarily require tearing down the walls. Wiring can be "fished" through walls from a small hole or section of the wall or ceiling.)

The Least You Need to Know

- Pay close attention to your electrical system, and address problems quickly to ensure safety.
- Aluminum wiring is generally considered a safety hazard and should be replaced.
- A qualified professional should do most electrical work; this isn't generally a do-it-yourself project.

Chapter 5

Heating and Air Conditioning

In This Chapter

- Different furnaces, different problems
- Backdrafting is bad news
- Be sure to clean the filter

Heating and air conditioning systems are essential parts of any home. It's more than just a matter of comfort; in many regions, heating is essential (at least for part of the year) to keep you alive. In warmer areas, air conditioning may also be vital for your health. There are many components of residential heating and air conditioning systems, so these systems will get considerable scrutiny during a home inspection.

Furnace Age and Condition

Make sure you note the age and general condition of your furnace. Using that info, you can research the normal expected life span of your particular type of furnace, which can give you a rough estimate of how much more life you can expect from your furnace.

Heat Exchangers

The heart and soul of a furnace is the heat exchanger, so obviously this is an area of major interest to a home inspector. The problem is, a considerable portion of the heat exchanger isn't easily visible. One common way of checking for possible problems is by watching for changes in the flame pattern. The flame should remain the same whether the fan is on or off. If the flame changes once the fan goes on, it could indicate a hole or crack in the heat exchanger. This presents a serious safety hazard, as it could allow lethal carbon monoxide fumes to leak into the home.

© *HouseMaster*

Changes in the heater flame can signal a problem.

The use of a mirror may be helpful in checking out the heat exchanger. Holding the mirror at various angles may help you see otherwise hidden areas of the exchanger. This will allow for greater visibility of the heat exchanger but is still no guarantee that you'll be able to spot every problem.

An experienced inspector will look for signs of corrosion and cracks; cracks may have developed in known "hot spots" on certain model furnaces or on welded sections known to crack. Experience and know-how will help. Still, it is a very difficult task.

Should there be any indications of a crack in the heat exchanger, heavy corrosion, or concerns with the burner, further evaluation will be required.

 Something to Dwell On _____

Heating equipment using gas or oil requires combustion gas. Units located in closets or small rooms without fresh air supply are a danger. Lack of combustion air leads to improper combustion at the burners, which results in carbon monoxide. Closet doors should be louvered or have other means of allowing fresh air in. Also, some installations such as garage locations require, in general, units to be raised off the floor, usually 18 inches. This will reduce the possibility of fire should some combustible liquid be spilled in the vicinity of the burner.

Oil Furnaces

Check your oil furnace's combustion chamber for cracks or other signs of deterioration. Note whether the burner flame is properly adjusted and positioned (it should be turned upward and not striking the back wall). The furnace's emergency shutoff switch should be easily accessible and clearly marked.

Gas Furnaces

Gas furnaces are very common in residential buildings. Many homeowners like the convenience of gas furnaces—there are no worries that you'll unexpectedly run out of fuel, as with oil furnaces. But gas furnaces do present their own specific maintenance and safety concerns.

The biggest concern, obviously, is the gas itself. Pay close attention to any signs of a possible gas leak. Should you suspect a gas leak, leave the home immediately and call the gas company or emergency personnel.

Nuts and Bolts _____

> The average life span of a gas or oil furnace is about 15 years. Average cost? $1,500 and up.

Inspectors cannot check the gas pressure of a furnace. They do, however, have equipment to check for combustible gas leaks, and they will also check the filter, the blower motor, burners, and venting/drafting. In some areas of the country, checking for carbon monoxide is routine but not part of any standard of practice.

Wood and Coal Furnaces

Although not as common as primary heat sources as they once were, wood and coal furnaces and heaters have become popular secondary heating sources.

The biggest problem is that, while few homeowners would think of tackling a furnace installation involving gas or oil burners, many wood and coal furnaces are installed by inexperienced homeowners who may not be familiar with safety procedures and other concerns.

Check to ensure that the wood or coal furnace was installed properly, paying careful attention to venting and safety clearances. If not, you may be violating local safety codes.

 Home Alarms

Run your furnace for a few minutes in late summer, before the cold weather hits. This will enable you to detect any problems while you still have time to fix them before you find yourself in a freezing house.

Common Problems: Furnace

There are a number of furnace-related problems to look for, including:

- Worn, damaged, or improperly installed parts. Small parts such as belts and filters are inexpensive and easy for a homeowner to install. Bigger parts such as a heat exchanger are quite costly and should be installed by a professional.

- Cracks or holes in the heat exchanger, a serious problem that needs to be checked by a professional. In many cases, the exchanger will need to be replaced. However, it may be more cost-efficient to replace the entire furnace. Because makes and models change frequently, there is very little chance in replacing a heat exchanger. You simply can't find the part and even if you could, paying $500 to $900 to replace a heat exchanger on a 12-year-old system does not make sense.

- Filters that are damaged or need to be replaced. These are cheap and easy to do yourself.

Check Those Air Filters!

Be sure to check your furnace's air filter regularly (for example, when you receive your electric bill), and change it as often as needed. This is a simple job you can do yourself, and filters cost about a buck. *Not* changing your filter, on the other hand, will cost you much more. Dirty filters force the furnace to work harder, increasing your energy bills. In addition, a dirty filter can damage your furnace or cause it to overheat. Worst-case scenario? You end up shelling out $2,000 or more for a new furnace simply because you were too lazy to change the filter.

 Nuts and Bolts _____

> A furnace or boiler's efficiency is measured by annual fuel utilization efficiency (AFUE). AFUE tells you how efficient the appliance is in using fuel or electricity over a typical year of use. The higher a furnace's AFUE, the more efficient it is—meaning the less you'll pay in utility bills to run it.

Heat Pumps

The heat pump is a system designed to capture heat—which can be found even in air that feels cold—and utilize it for home heating. An electric compressor pumps a refrigerant between coils outside the house and in ductwork inside the house. During cold weather, as the refrigerant moves from outdoors to inside, it absorbs heat and releases it inside the house. This warmed air is then distributed throughout the house via the ductwork.

Heat pumps are really only economical at moderately cold temperatures. To handle very low temperatures, most heat pumps would need supplemental coils. The use of these supplemental coils will result in a significant jump in utility costs to operate the heat pump.

High-Efficiency Heating Systems

High-efficiency heating systems are quickly becoming the standard for new homes and replacement units in existing homes. The term "high efficiency" covers a wide range of systems with varying installation requirements. It's common to use plastic venting piping for these units.

For these systems to work properly, it's essential that condensation be controlled to prevent damage to the heat exchanger or venting system.

High-efficiency heating systems should only be installed by a qualified professional and should be checked regularly. The inspector will look for signs of condensation buildup or damage to the exchanger or vents.

Venting

The metal pipe connecting an appliance to a chimney or exhausting outside is called a vent. Fuel-burning appliances exhaust the products of combustion to the exterior through vent pipes. Vent pipes that are damaged, clogged, or too short may result in inadequate or poor drafting.

Also, a vent can be connected to a chimney flue as long as the flue serving the fireplace is not connected to the heating system flue. They must be sealed off from one another within the chimney and the opening of the fireplace flue where it exits the chimney must be far enough away from the heating system flue to eliminate the chance of backdrafting.

Look for rust holes and other damage to the vents and connector pipes. Be sure not to block any air vents around or near your heating system. Also, a vent must not be connected to a chimney flue serving a fireplace unless the fireplace opening is sealed or the flue serving the fireplace is permanently sealed below the connection.

 Home Alarms

It's important to have your heating/cooling system checked yearly by a qualified heating professional. A home inspection is a good general evaluation, but should not be used as a substitute for an annual heating inspection. Have the furnace checked—preferably before cold weather hits—to prevent carbon monoxide leaks and other potential problems and to give yourself enough time to make any necessary repairs. A yearly heating/cooling tune-up costs around $100, and the contractor will usually also check/change air filters and check coolant levels.

We'll talk more about ventilation involving chimneys and fireplaces in Chapter 11. And as we mentioned in Chapter 2, proper attic ventilation is important to prevent heat and moisture buildup, which could cause roof damage.

Baseboard, Radiators, and Other Distribution Systems

Most heating systems utilize some method of distributing heat to various parts of the home. Forced-air heaters use ducts and registers. Water heating systems use pipes and radiators or convectors, while radiant systems may use pipes or wires. A radiant system may use pipes embedded in the floors or wires or radiant panels on or in ceilings, etc.

Since much of the distribution system—and related potential problems—are not visible, you can't spend a lot of time evaluating these components. Obviously, you'll notice if a radiator doesn't get hot or isn't working at all. Noisy radiators or baseboards are often a sign of air in the lines, meaning that you may need to *bleed the pipes*.

House Keys

Bleeding the pipes refers to the process of opening the valves—slowly and carefully—to let excess air escape.

If a room isn't getting warm enough, you may need to add an additional baseboard, which will cost you around $200 and is something most home handymen and women can handle.

The Bottom Line on Heating

Furnaces and heaters consist of many different parts, ranging from small and inexpensive to big and pricey. For a small, inexpensive part, replacement is usually the way to go. With more expensive parts, repair—although probably cheaper than replacement—might not be the best route.

For example, if your heat exchanger suffers major damage, it most likely will be beyond repair and will need to be replaced. In fact, at that point you might want to consider replacing the entire furnace.

- Change filter (do it yourself): around $1
- Install high-efficiency boiler: $5,000 and up
- Install new oil furnace: $1,500 and up
- Install new gas furnace: $1,750 to $3,000
- Add new baseboard (do it yourself): $200 to $300
- Install programmable thermostat (yourself): $25 to $125

Nuts and Bolts

HVAC refers to Heating, Ventilation, and Air Conditioning.

Central Air Conditioning

Central air conditioning is a standard feature in many new homes, and is a necessity in very warm climates. Like furnaces, air conditioning units seem to have a knack for breaking down at the worst possible times (say, during a heat wave), so it's wise to try and spot potential problems early.

The *compressor* is the most expensive and important part of a cooling system (see the figure that follows). The *evaporator coil* is also a vital part of the air conditioning unit.

© HouseMaster

An air conditioning compressor.

House Keys

The **compressor** circulates coolant through the air conditioning unit. The **evaporator coil** absorbs heat from the air prior to it entering the cooled space.

You can—and should—check and replace your air conditioner's filter and coolant yourself. However, repairing or replacing major parts like a compressor should be done by a professional.

How much will it cost for you to keep your cool?

- Average life span of air conditioning unit: 10 to 15 years
- Air conditioning compressor: $800 to $1200 and up
- Adding central air conditioning on an existing forced-air system: $2,500 to $3,000

Operating Controls (Thermostats)

Operating controls related to heating and cooling generally consist of some kind of thermostat. Watch for thermostats that are loose, cracked, or otherwise visibly damaged.

Turning down your thermostat at night can slash up to 15 percent off your home heating bills, but most people don't do it—usually because they simply forget. A programmable thermostat can solve this problem. You can program it to lower the temperature after you're sleeping, and raise it in the morning so you'll awake to a toasty house. A programmable thermostat is something the average person can install themselves, but the savings in energy cost make it a bargain even if you pay someone else to do it. Programmable thermostats cost $25 to $125 (it'll probably cost you at least $200 for a contractor to do it).

The Least You Need to Know

- Watch out for gas leaks, pressure buildups, and backdrafting.

- Spend a buck and five minutes changing the filter, and you'll avoid big problems down the road.

- A programmable thermostat can save you big bucks.

- Heating systems should be checked annually by a qualified repairman to avoid costly— and possibly dangerous—problems.

- The compressor is the most important and most expensive part of an air conditioning unit.

Doors and Windows

In This Chapter

- Don't ignore your doors
- Watch out for window worries
- When little cracks mean big problems

A home's doors and windows are kind of like the "front line," the outer shell that covers and protects the home inside. Like any exposed feature, those parts of a home are especially vulnerable to damage from weather, accidental mishaps, and other problems.

In many ways, you play detective when examining a home's doors and windows. Many of a home's important elements are concealed underneath floors, and are therefore not visible to actual inspection. So, you must look for visible clues of a problem that may be lurking out of sight.

Entry Doors

Entry doors keep precious things like kids and pets (along with expensive stuff like heat and energy) indoors, while keeping intruders and the elements out.

Note the type and general condition of your entry doors. While interior doors are often hollow core, entry doors should be solid and sturdy.

Interior Doors

Note the number and location of interior doors. Watch for holes, splintering, or other signs of damage. The doors should open and close easily, and the hinges and any locks should be in good working order.

When evaluating doors, look for binding doors and out-of-plumb jambs. These conditions may be evidence of underlying structural concerns. Foundation and framing support concerns will result in binding doors.

Sliding Doors

Sliding doors are susceptible to leakage, especially if they aren't installed properly. Check to make sure the doors slide back and forth easily, with no sticking or jamming. Also see if the doors fit snugly against the frame, and watch out for cracks or other areas where leaks can occur.

The average double-glazed slider door costs from $800 to $2000 (installed).

Storm/Screen Doors

Many home inspectors do not evaluate screen and/
or storm doors as part of their routine service, but
you should keep an eye out for obvious problems
such as cracked panes, torn screens, and broken
hinges.

A typical combination screen/storm door costs $200
to $500 and can be installed by the homeowner.

Common Problems: Doors

Common door-related problems include frames
that are warped or not square (out of *plumb*), doors
that don't close tightly, hinges or locks that are broken or missing, and weatherstripping that is damaged. Wood that is damaged, splintered, or rotting
can also be a problem, along with cracked or broken panels or panes.

The Bottom Line on Doors

Entry doors can cost $300 or more. Wood doors
are generally cheaper than steel doors, but wooden
doors are more susceptible to sagging or damage,
and offer less insulation than steel doors.

Interior doors generally cost less than $50 for hol-
low core varieties, and higher for solid wood. If the
door has a large hole, crack, or other damage, it's
usually more practical to simply replace the entire
door than to try to repair it.

The cost also depends on the quality of the door, and whether you buy a door that is *pre-hung* or unassembled.

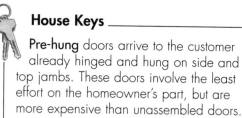

House Keys

Pre-hung doors arrive to the customer already hinged and hung on side and top jambs. These doors involve the least effort on the homeowner's part, but are more expensive than unassembled doors.

Plain flat doors will usually be much cheaper than doors with panels or other fancy details.

The good news is that the average homeowner can handle virtually all door-related repairs and installations. Also, a $10 tube of caulking may be all you need to eliminate some minor gaps or draft problems.

Windows

Look for obvious problems, such as cracked or broken windows and torn screens. Note any windows that do not open easily, are painted shut, or do not remain open without assistance. Window frames should not have cracks or holes, or otherwise be vulnerable to leaks. The window should fit snugly in its frame, and the weatherstripping and/or insulation should be in good condition. Examine the window sill and trim for rot or other signs of damage.

Home Alarms _____

> As with out-of-plumb door jambs, windows that are out of plumb may be a sign of structural concerns.

Hung windows are the traditional type of windows featuring two panels, where either the lower sash or, in the case of double-hung windows, the lower and upper sashes open and close. Years ago, hung windows used ropes or chains to support the sashes, but modern windows use springs. If the home features older windows, check the condition of the ropes or chains, as they have a tendency to fray or break, presenting a safety risk of the window slamming down unexpectedly.

Nuts and Bolts _____

> A double-hung window opens from both the top and bottom. Casement windows have hinges on the side and open in a manner similar to a door. The window pane is the actual piece of glass, and the sash is the portion of the window that slides or turns when the window is opened and closed.

Double-Pane Windows

A double-pane window features two sheets of glass, with an area (ranging from $1/2$ inch to an inch) of dead space between the panes.

This provides greater energy efficiency and reduces heat loss. However, these windows are prone to problems relating to manufacturer defects or improper installation.

A common problem involves moisture getting between the panes and condensing inside the window, ultimately producing a stained or dirty look. The space between the panes is a vacuum, but if the seal is broken, air is drawn in. The moisture in the air condenses on the inside of the window. Technically, this is a failure of the window requiring replacement. There's no way to really "fix" this problem, so replacement is usually the only real solution.

Storm Windows

Again, look for obvious problems such as cracks, holes, and leaks. Storm windows generally cost $75 to $125 each, and you can install them yourself. Generally, storm windows are left on the window year-round—you simply pull them down so they cover the window and help prevent drafts during cold weather.

Common Problems: Windows

There are several common window-related problems, including:

- Windows that are painted shut or otherwise do not open.
- Broken sash ropes or chains.

- Cracked window panes.
- Leaks.
- Weatherstripping that is damaged or missing.
- Broken window seals.
- Damaged locks and hardware.

Window panes and weatherstripping can usually be repaired. However, windows that have broken ropes or leaks, or that do not fit properly in their frames, may need to be completely replaced.

The Bottom Line on Windows

Windows have an average life span of 15 to 20 years (less, if you have aspiring baseball players in your neighborhood or live near a golf course). This is a good thing, because windows can be surprisingly expensive. With windows generally running anywhere from $200 to $700 or more apiece, it's very common for a homeowner to spend thousands of dollars on new windows. On the positive side, an inexpensive tube of caulk can often lessen or eliminate minor drafts, leaks, and other window concerns.

While window costs vary widely, unusual shapes or sizes, energy-efficiency properties, or other special features will all increase the price.

Average Costs:

Replace standard double-pane window: $200 to $400 each

Replace broken glass: $30 to $50 per window

Potential Underlying Problems with Doors and Windows

The biggest concern with problems involving windows and doors is that buckles and cracks can be a symptom of a much bigger—and scarier—problem: underlying structural damage. Repairing a major structural problem can easily cost you $8,000 to $15,000 or more. A major structural problem can also be a serious safety hazard. This is why you should watch for any seemingly small problems—such as cracks around doors and windows—and consult a structural engineer or other qualified professional at the first sign of trouble.

The Least You Need to Know

- You can do most repairs and installations involving doors and windows yourself.
- The price of doors can vary widely, depending on material and style.
- Windows can be surprisingly costly, so you should take care to properly maintain and protect them.
- Your doors and windows can warn you about possible structural problems.

Walls, Floors, Ceilings, and Stairs

In This Chapter

- Watch out for faulty floors
- Stairs can be scary
- Your walls can speak volumes

The walls and floors of your home serve as a buffer to keep everything in your home cozy and insulated—even from other rooms within the home. But walls and floors also serve as an alarm system, often displaying telltale signs that a structural problem may be lurking in hidden areas of your home.

Walls

In older homes, walls often featured a plaster coat covering a lath base made of wood (see the following figure), rock, or metal. Today, most walls are made with drywall, which greatly speeds up the construction process and is cheaper and easier to install than the older materials.

Walls frequently contain a wood base, especially in older homes.

The common problems associated with walls are cracks, peeling paint, and water stains. These may sound like purely cosmetic defects, but big cracks— especially near windows and doors—may signal structural problems. It's not unusual for homes to shift and settle over time, but walls that have been recently painted or tiled and have already cracked are signs of a recent problem.

Walls may also lean or bulge, which again would probably point to a bigger problem.

Simple cracks or peeling paint can be pretty easy and inexpensive to fix. Bigger problems, such as walls that sag or lean, can involve some major expenses.

Lead Paint

Lead paint—often found in older homes—has been shown to be hazardous, especially to kids. If you have an older home, watch for signs of lead paint on the walls and windows. The only way to permanently fix a lead paint problem is to have all traces of the paint completely removed.

Something to Dwell On

Federal legislation requires all home sellers to disclose (in writing) that if the house was built before 1978 it may contain lead-based paint. Real-estate agents usually facilitate the paperwork—they can be held accountable if the buyer does not receive a disclosure form. Even if you are not using an agent, the disclosure must take place. Buyers should be aware that the seller is under no obligation, legally or otherwise, to remove or repair any concerns relative to lead paint. The law is to provide the buyer with information only. Because the disclosure must take place when the seller accepts the buyer's offer, the home inspector has absolutely no obligation or duty to mention or report on lead-based paint.

The Bottom Line on Walls

Cosmetic wall problems like cracks and holes are among the most common home repair projects.

Most homeowners can easily handle a paintbrush and some spackle. Don't want to do it yourself? Here's what you can expect to pay:

- Installing drywall over plaster: $2 to $3 per square foot
- Patching or plastering damaged area: $5 to $12 per square foot
- Installing paneling: $2 to $6.50 per square foot

Floors

Your main concerns when it comes to floors are sagging, sloping, and other signs of unevenness. This is more common in older homes, and tends to get progressively worse as wooden beams continue to age.

The most common floor problem is unevenness in the form of sloping or sagging. A sag or dip in one small spot may indicate a minor defect in the floor. But if the entire floor area is sloped, it may signal a bigger structural problem. We will address problems specifically relating to garage floors, patios, and driveways in Chapter 10.

Other common problems include cracked or split hardwood flooring and torn or damaged carpeting. Small dips or sags in a floor may require simply fixing or replacing a small portion of the floor. A severely sloping floor, however, could indicate structural problems that may be expensive to rectify—think $5,000 or considerably more. Most homeowners can install adhesive vinyl flooring squares themselves, but carpeting, tile, and hardwood flooring generally require the skills and/or tools of a professional.

Floor costs:

- Refinish hardwood floor: $.50 to $1.25 per square foot
- Replace hardwood floor: $8 to $14 per square foot
- Carpet installation: $20 to $45 per square yard
- Tile installation: $20 to $45 per square foot

Nuts and Bolts

If a home inspector is concerned that problems with the floors, walls, or ceilings may signal a bigger problem, he or she will recommend further evaluation by an engineer or other specialist qualified to check the home's structural integrity.

Ceilings

Note the general condition of the ceiling, paying close attention to water stains or other signs of leaks, cracks, and peeling paint. Small cracks and peeling paint are minor defects that can be relatively easy to fix. Major cracks, however, can be signs of a structural problem that requires the attention of an engineer or other specialist. Although water stains may be easy to cover, you should still pay attention to them, as they signal a leak that needs to be addressed.

While the work involved in doing basic ceiling repairs is probably within the abilities of a basic homeowner, you may need to hire someone if special equipment is needed—for example, if your ceilings are high or hard to reach, or if you want special features such as textured or "popcorn" ceilings.

Ceiling repair costs:

- Add dropped ceiling: $3 to $5 per square foot
- Paint ceiling: 60 cents per square foot (texturing and other special features are extra)

Stairs

The stairway is one of the most dangerous spots in your house. Stairs that are broken, uneven, loose, or weak can all spell potential disaster. Watch for steps that are too narrow or too closely spaced, as well as steps that are damaged or broken. Carpet or other covering should be smooth and secure, with no bulges or gaps that might present a tripping hazard.

A single damaged step is something that you can probably repair yourself quickly and cheaply. On the other hand, a stairway that has major deterioration, several broken steps, or steps that are uneven or too narrow will probably need to be completely replaced. If you have some carpentry skills, you may want to try doing this yourself. Otherwise, hire a contractor. Figure at least $400 for a basic set of indoor steps.

The Biggest Concern, Again

As we mentioned in Chapter 6, the biggest concern with problems involving walls and floors (as with windows and doors) is that slopes, buckles, and cracks can be a symptom of underlying structural damage, which can easily cost you thousands of dollars.

The Least You Need to Know

- Minor wall repairs are an easy do-it-yourself job.
- Stairs are an accident hotspot, so make sure your stairways are a risk-free zone.
- A floor that slopes completely may signal structural problems and should be investigated ASAP.

Chapter 8

Basements, Foundations, Land, and Property

In This Chapter

- Don't take your foundation for granted
- Why poor drainage can spell disaster
- Reading the cracks on your basement walls

You wouldn't build a million-dollar mansion on quicksand, would you? Of course not, but do you really know how secure the "roots" of your home are? A family needs a solid foundation—literally. The rest of your home could be totally perfect, but if it's resting on top of a bad foundation or has other structural problems, the whole home could be in jeopardy.

So, when evaluating your home, it's important to get to the bottom of things, and thoroughly check out your foundation and basement as well as any related issues outdoors. Perhaps the biggest property and foundation concern (and a common theme throughout this chapter) is water. Yes, water is essential for life, but it's deadly to your basement and foundation. So, we'll spend a good portion of this chapter telling you how water can hurt your home and, more importantly, how you can prevent water damage without spending a fortune.

Land and Property

Home inspectors don't spend a large chunk of time evaluating the land and property, because—with a few exceptions, such as drainage and vegetation—land-related issues don't really fall under a home inspector's jurisdiction. The majority of property-related issues—such as septic systems, insects, and underground oil tanks—would need to be handled by a specialist such as an exterminator or septic contractor.

Boundaries and Property Lines

A home inspector won't locate or measure your property lines or verify your boundaries. If that's something you need done, you should consult a surveyor.

Retaining Walls

You should evaluate any *retaining walls* on the property for signs of deterioration or other unsafe conditions. If a property is steeply sloped and water runoff is a concern, adding retaining walls may help the property level off somewhat, reducing direct runoff to the house.

Expect to pay $12 to $30 per square foot for a typical retaining wall.

> **House Keys**
>
> A **retaining wall** is a boundary, usually several feet high and commonly made of stone, designed to keep water or soil from encroaching (intruding on) on a property.

Drainage

Perhaps the most common problem revealed in home inspections is poor drainage.

Proper drainage is important for keeping your property well maintained. Water penetration can cause soil to erode and become unstable, and can lead to foundation problems. Plus, this can cause flooding, which would damage the basement and possibly destroy your stuff. Also, in a wood frame home, constant dampness can lead to rot and can also attract termites and other damaging insects.

See the photo that follows for an example of a basement wall that lacks proper water protection.

Look for signs of poor drainage, which will usually be pretty obvious. Standing pools of water that remain long after a storm has ended could be a red flag. Water that flows heavily toward the home would also be cause for concern. During a heavy rain, it may be beneficial to go outside and observe all potential conditions that may contribute to seepage concerns.

© HouseMaster

Lack of proper moisture protection can cause big problems.

The good news is, by taking a proactive approach to drainage and addressing concerns early (or before you even notice a problem) you can usually take the cheaper, easier route. On the other hand, if you wait until drainage problems become severe, it might already be too late to avoid major foundation damage (meaning, major repair costs).

Solutions for a drainage problem include installing drains and/or gutters and making landscaping changes that will allow water to flow away from the house.

Installing gutters is a fairly involved and strenuous project. While a homeowner may attempt small section repairs, the most common type of gutter—seamless—is made on-site using special equipment that forms the one-piece gutter out of flat aluminum sheets.

Related costs:

- New aluminum gutters: $3.50 to $5.50 per foot
- Downspouts: $3 to $4.50 per foot
- Average life span of gutters/downspouts: 15 to 30 years

We'll talk more about gutters in Chapter 12.

Grading

When evaluating the property grade, you should make sure water is directed away from the home. Proper grading is one of the easiest and most effective ways to ensure good drainage, reducing or eliminating the possibility of costly water damage.

If the house is situated on a slope in which water runs toward the house, small *swales* can be an option to solve the water problem. A few well-designed swales can divert the water away from the house. Perimeter drains can also help prevent water from accumulating. Unless you have landscaping equipment and experience, it's probably best to hire an expert to handle this.

Prices vary greatly, depending on how much time and equipment is required, but if the job requires a backhoe or other heavy equipment, you can expect to pay at least $500 a day. Perimeter drains will usually cost around $25 per foot.

> **House Keys**
>
> A **swale** is an impression in the ground designed to divert water away from the home.

Vegetation

There are a few concerns related to vegetation that you should look for. Vegetation growing on or very close to the home can cause all sorts of problems—insects, mold, and rodents, to name a few. Also, certain types of trees tend to have large root systems that can damage a home's foundation or septic system.

Another problem with excessive vegetation near the home is that it can conceal other problems, so you wouldn't be able to spot trouble brewing until it becomes a big problem.

The good news is, you can treat many vegetation problems yourself, with basic equipment such as garden shears or a weed cutter.

For bigger problems, such as large root systems, you'll probably need to hire a professional.

Foundations

The *foundation* is basically the base of your home. It's the thing that holds the rest of your home up, so obviously it's pretty important. It's a major part of a home's construction, and that—along with the fact that it has a house sitting on top of it—can make a foundation costly to repair. Still, when it comes to foundation concerns, you can't procrastinate. If there is a serious problem with the foundation, the integrity of your entire home's structure—not to mention the safety of anyone in it—could be at risk. That's why it's important to keep an eye out for problems and to address them as early as possible.

House Keys

The **foundation** is a wall, usually made from some form of masonry material, on which the house's framing is built. The foundation provides structural support and is one of the most critical parts of a home or building. The **footer** (or **footing**) is the concrete base that the foundation sits on.

Most foundations are made from some type of masonry product—block, brick, poured concrete, or even rock. These foundations have many similarities, and there are several red flags such as cracking, erosion, and shifting that are common to all of them.

Then there are "slab" foundations, which consist of a concrete floor poured into a perimeter foundation made up of a footing and foundation of block or concrete. The foundation comes up to grade only. The concrete pad poured into this serves as the first floor of the house. Slab foundations have their own problems—water is one, but so are expansive soils such as clay that cause the slab to heave and buckle. In the southwest they are very common. Basement walls would collapse in those conditions.

Common Problems: Foundations

As we've already mentioned, water damage is probably the most common—and most harmful—foundation concern.

You should also keep an eye out for cracks and other signs of possible structural damage. Although a structural engineer should check any foundation concerns, there are a few hints that may help you determine if you have a serious problem.

Horizontal Cracks

The cause of a horizontal crack is horizontal load or pressure on the wall from the outside, usually water pressure or expansive soils. The result is that the wall is not properly bearing the house load vertically from top to bottom. Did you ever sit at a bar and play with the swizzle stick in your vodka and tonic? When you add pressure to the ends of the stick, it starts to bend or bow; give enough pressure and it collapses. Same thing happens with a wall. So horizontal cracks come from horizontal pressure on the wall. This can even sometimes be traced back to improper backfilling of the foundation trench when the house was built.

Generally, only a structural engineer can identify the cause of the problem. Solutions can be costly, and usually involve adding some type of reinforcement such as piers or additional supporting walls.

Diagonal Cracks

Diagonal cracks are usually a result of differential settlement. This means that the crack is a result of one corner of a house foundation settling slightly more than the other. It is generally no cause for concern unless the crack develops into something more than $1/8$ inch. It is not a technical wall failure, as with horizontal cracks. It may simply be "normal" settling.

The Price of Foundation Problems

Foundation problems can be costly, and they're generally not a "do-it-yourself" project. But it's important to get foundation concerns addressed quickly by a qualified professional, to prevent the damage from getting worse and possibly putting the entire home in jeopardy.

Also, if your insurance company feels that you did not properly address drainage concerns, they can refuse to cover water-related foundation damages.

Here's what you can expect to pay to address some common foundation problems:

- Add piers to existing foundation: $500 to $800 each
- Rebuild foundation wall: $100/foot
- Reinforce foundation corner: $1,000 and up

> **Something to Dwell On** _____
>
> A finished basement can increase a home's value considerably, in addition to providing valuable added living space. It'll generally cost you around $15,000 to hire someone to finish an existing basement. If you have some handyman skills, you could probably do it yourself for about half that.

Basement Floors and Walls

Again, when evaluating a basement, you want to be particularly alert for any signs of water penetration. A musty smell or water marks near the base of foundation walls are common red flags. In finished basements, loose floor tiles can often mean water damage.

We've already explained in great detail why water can be a big problem for foundations and basements. But Mother Nature isn't the only source of water. Keep an eye out for leaks and other plumbing problems in the basement.

Crawl Space

Crawl spaces are small, unfinished spaces, usually found underneath the home or in the attic. They're generally used just for storage. Check your crawl space for standing puddles or other signs of water penetration (see the following photo).

© *HouseMaster*

Keep an eye out for moisture problems in crawl spaces.

 **Home Alarms**

Use extreme caution when exploring crawl spaces. Exposed wiring can be dangerous, especially if there's standing water. There may also be loose or disconnected pipes that could fall on you. Plus, crawl spaces are popular homes for rodents and other furry creatures. You don't want to be crouched in a dark crawl space and suddenly encounter a pair of eyes staring back at you.

Sump Pumps

A sump pump is an electric pump (although battery-powered "back-up" models are also available) that is usually installed in a sump pit. Piping may have been installed under the concrete basement floor that is also connected to the foundation wall. As water enters through the wall, it is diverted through the pipes (French Drain) into the sump pit. The sump pump pumps it out of the house and away from the foundation.

In some homes, the sump pit is not connected to underfloor piping and is designed to catch surface water runoff. The water is pumped out in a similar fashion. Things to be concerned about include the sump pump discharging into the public sewer line and, even worse, into the private septic system. Also, if you do not pump the water far enough away from the foundation, it may just flow back into the house and re-circulate through the system again.

Costs:

- Sump pump and pit: around $500
- Replace existing sump pump: $250

The Least You Need to Know

- A home inspector won't measure or verify your boundaries or property lines.
- Proper drainage is extremely important in preventing major structural damage.
- Serious problems in the foundation can be very expensive to repair.

Bathrooms and Kitchens

In This Chapter

- Trouble with tubs and toilets
- Sizing up the shower pan
- Keeping your kitchen in good shape

The bathroom and kitchen are two of the most heavily used parts of the home. They are also where you'll find lots of appliances, plumbing, and other features that are prone to problems and damage.

Bathroom

Pretty much everything in a bathroom is somehow connected to water, so one big priority when evaluating a bathroom is checking for leaks, mold, sagging floors, and other signs of water problems.

Walls and Ceilings

The first item to consider is the overall appearance of the walls and ceilings as a clue to underlying structural integrity of the covered framing. Ceiling stains may indicate plumbing stack flashing concerns. Peeling paint may be a sign of mildew or mold or may indicate moisture problems due to venting problems.

Floors

Carefully check floors for signs of water or structural damage. Improper cutting of floor framing to accommodate pipe installation is not uncommon. This leads to structural settlement. Sponginess or movement of the floor at the base of the toilet may indicate a failure in the wax ring, which helps seal the pipe connection.

Tiles

Tiled walls in bathrooms are very popular with homeowners these days, but they are prone to problems. Keep an eye out for loose or missing ceramic tiles and deteriorating grout. Tapping on the tiles may find loose tiles in areas. Tile repairs will often require wall repairs.

© HouseMaster

Missing tiles are a common bathroom problem.

Bathtub

The bathtub should be sturdy, with no cracks or other signs of damage. An unsturdy tub is usually pretty obvious—if you can rock back and forth as if on a boat while taking a bath, that's a bad sign. Caulking around the tub should be adequate to prevent leaks or water penetration (see the following figure).

© HouseMaster

Watch out for leaks near whirlpools.

Shower Stall

A shower stall is an enclosed unit that contains only a shower (as opposed to combination shower/tub units).

Shower enclosures should be properly caulked and maintained to avoid leakage. Glass panels should be the tempered safety-glass variety.

It is not uncommon for enclosures to be added on over old, damaged tiles and walls (see the following figure). The enclosure should be thoroughly checked for cracks in addition to proper caulking.

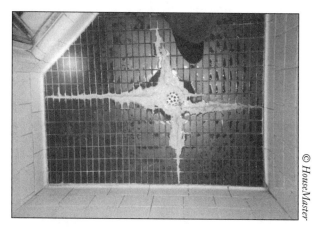

A badly cracked shower floor can be a safety hazard.

Shower Pan

A shower pan is basically the bottom-most part of the shower assembly. It's located under the floor tiles or concrete base of a shower. Often made of metal, tile, or plastic, the shower pan basically keeps water from going where it shouldn't. A broken or defective shower pan can be a big, expensive problem, as it can lead to water damage of the subfloor and framing.

Windows

Windows located in tub or shower areas may lead to problems. Windows should be properly protected against moisture to avoid the costly consequences of moisture-related damage.

A Few Important Details

While we're on the subject of bathrooms, we want to take a moment to mention two important bathroom-related details:

- Heat source: You would be surprised at how may people forget to include a heat source when planning a bathroom remodel. Cold toilets and cold mornings don't go together—take our word for it. Plus, heat is important for keeping pipes from freezing during winter.

- Electric: We can't say enough about the importance of GFCI outlets. Check out more on GFCI in Chapter 4.

Sink

Check to make sure the faucets work properly and aren't loose or broken. Look under the sink for signs of leaks. Run the sink and the bathtub faucets at the same time, to see if water pressure is affected.

Check under the sink, look for leaks, and locate the fixture shut-off valves. Inspect the condition of the piping and determine if a drain trap is present.

Fixtures

Vanity tops should be checked for wear and tear, chipping, and cracking. Medicine cabinets should be properly secured.

Toilet

The most common toilet-related problem is leakage from the wax ring (see the figure that follows). Pay careful attention to the base of the toilet, as this is a common area for leaks.

Flush the toilet and watch for leaks or drips. Also make sure that the unit flushes properly and fills to the proper level. Listen to make sure that the tank refills properly. The water should not continue to run (this can cause your water bills to soar).

Check to see if it is properly bolted to the floor, and not loose and rocking. Check for cracking of the bowl and tank cover.

Keep an eye out for leaks and other toilet troubles.

Signs of Trouble

Watch for mold, water stains, sagging floors, rippled walls, and other red flags that might indicate water damage. Also look for loose or missing tiles, which can allow water to damage the walls and floors.

Make sure the toilet is secure and shows no signs of leaks.

Drains that gurgle or empty very slowly can be a sign of plumbing problems.

Bathroom Ventilation

With all the heat and moisture found in bathrooms (especially if your family is fond of hot showers), proper ventilation is critical to preventing mold and rot. The minimal requirement is a window only. If a fan is present, it should be ducted directly to the exterior.

 Home Alarms

If you have a vent leading from the bathroom to outside, be sure it has screening or a flap to keep things from coming *in*. For some reason, bats are very fond of these vents, and that's one thing you don't want to see zooming around the bathroom ceiling while you're in the shower.

The majority of vent-related problems involve the "exit" end of the vent. Sometimes vents do not lead outside, but rather to an attic or other part of the home. This simply relocates the problem, as the heat and moisture are then likely to damage that part of the home.

The Bottom Line on Bathrooms

Common bathroom expenses:

- Replace shower pan: $1,000 to $1,500
- Reset Toilet: $100 to $250

Kitchen

Evaluate the kitchen for general overall safety. Pay particular attention to anything that might present a fire hazard or otherwise be a safety concern. Check to make sure smoke detectors are working properly. A nearby fire extinguisher would also be a plus.

Kitchen Ventilation

Major cooking appliances require an adequate vent system. Fans really aren't that effective in removing heat and moisture. Check to see if your appliances are vented outside or through a filtered (micro-hood) system.

GFCI Outlets

Ground fault circuit interrupters are required on all receptacles serving a kitchen counter.

Sink

The sink should be firmly secured to the countertop. The surface should be in good condition and relatively free or corrosion, scratches, and other damage. Faucet should be in good working order. Check underneath the sink for leaks.

Oven/Stove

The stove should have a vent or fan system in good working order. The stovetop should be clear and free of grease. All knobs, handles, and controls should be in good condition. The operating controls will be visually evaluated, but normally an inspector won't check the temperature accuracy.

Refrigerator

Look for signs of leakage on the floor near the fridge. There should be some leeway on the back and sides of the fridge to allow for air circulation. Inspectors may not typically inspect the fridge, since it often goes with the seller when a home changes hands. (The same is true of washers and dryers.)

 Home Alarms

Plugging your fridge into a GFCI is asking for trouble. You will only know all too late that it has tripped, causing all of your filet mignons and lobster tails to become ruined.

Garbage Disposal

Check to see that the disposal works properly and isn't excessively noisy. Make sure the control switch works properly. While they are usually turned on during an inspection, the effectiveness can't be determined because an inspector won't try to put anything down a garbage disposal.

Dishwashers

Run a built-in dishwasher through a complete cycle, watching for leaks or other signs of trouble.

Cabinets and Countertops

Look for loose or unstable cabinets. Keep an eye out for cracked or damaged countertops, as well, although these are generally just cosmetic problems.

Common Problems: Kitchens

Watch out for these common kitchen pitfalls:

- No GFCI outlets
- Appliances connected to receptacles not designed to handle those power requirements
- Refrigerator that leaks or doesn't sufficiently maintain temperature
- Improper (or nonexistent) vent systems

Home Alarms

Although a routine home inspection generally doesn't include an insect evaluation, a home inspector may be able to point out telltale signs of carpenter ants in the kitchen. These big black pests are attracted by food, and live in damp wood—meaning that kitchen cabinets (especially if they're prone to moisture) are the perfect haven for carpenter ants, which can be destructive (not to mention creepy).

The Least You Need to Know

- GCFI outlets can be a lifesaver in the bathroom and kitchen.

- Keep a close eye on your shower pan to avoid costly repair bills.

- Appliances are only checked for visible problems—an inspector can't say if your dishwasher will make your plates sparkle.

Chapter

Garages, Driveways, Porches, and Patios

In This Chapter

- Don't let your garage endanger your home
- Driveway drainage is important
- Why you should care about cantilevered balconies

Although a home inspector doesn't spend a lot of time on land and property concerns, there are still many exterior components that he or she will evaluate. Garages, driveways, porches, and patios are all usually included in routine home inspections.

Garages

If you're like most people these days, you probably feel like you live in your car. As a result, you may spend quite a bit of time in your garage. In addition, many people use their garage as a workshop, storage area, and so on, so it's important to keep this area safe and well maintained.

Vehicle Door

The vehicle doors should open and close easily. Unless they have an automatic opener, vehicle doors should have a lock. Look for damage or loose weatherstripping around the door. Door springs should be near the ceiling or otherwise located where they're unlikely to pinch someone's fingers. Springs should have a cable or other safety retainer as a "back-up," to prevent injury or damage in case the spring breaks.

Wooden doors are susceptible to moisture, so look for rot, peeling paint, or other signs of water damage. This is especially likely at the bottom of the door and on the surrounding trim.

Automatic Openers

Garage doors should stop immediately if something blocks their movement. Most modern garage-door systems are equipped with an automatic reverse control, which makes the door back up if it strikes something, or in some cases, if something blocks the path of the beam of light.

Garage Floor

Check the general condition of the garage floor. Most garage floors are made of concrete, and small cracks are fairly common, but large or continually growing cracks are cause for concern.

Evaluate the garage foundation. With an attached garage, the foundation should appear to be in roughly the same condition as that of the home. The foundation should not be pulling away from the house, and should not show more signs of settlement than the home.

Garage Ceiling and Roof

You would watch for the same problems on a garage roof that you would on the roof of the home. Water damage, missing or damaged shingles and other materials, and animal damage and infestation are all common garage roof problems.

Something to Dwell On

Garages are either attached (connected to the home or contained within the home) or unattached. Attached garages are more convenient—you can get from your car to your house without braving the elements. The downside to an attached garage, though, is that it exposes your home to potential hazards such as fire and carbon-monoxide fumes.

Connection to Living Area

With an attached garage, you should pay close attention to the door connecting the garage and the home. This is the only barrier protecting your home and family from possible hazards in the garage.

A steel or solid wood door is recommended. The door should fit tightly. Also, walls that the home and garage share should contain added insulation, a masonry firewall, or some other type of fire protection.

Water Heaters and Other Mechanical Equipment

Any water heaters or similar equipment in the garage must be at least 18 inches off the floor, and a shutoff switch should be easily accessible. In some cases, a vent may be needed for a gas water heater.

Electrical Concerns

Garage receptacles should be equipped with GFCI outlets. Outlets should be adequate in number and power to handle all garage needs without the frequent use of extension cords.

 Home Alarms

> Fuel and other flammable or combustible materials should be properly stored, and should be safely distanced from cars, heaters, or other possible sources of sparks.

Common Problems: Garages

The most common garage problems include the following:

- Vehicle door that doesn't stop/reverse properly
- Wood-destroying insect infestation (likely since the framing is built on or very close to the ground)
- Electricity in detached structures that may have been added by a homeowner and is typically not up to current standards
- Roof damage and leaks

The Bottom Line on Garages

Here's what you can expect to pay for common garage repairs/projects:

- Replace single wooden garage door: $500 to $1,000
- Install automatic garage door opener: $250 to $500

Driveways and Walkways

Inspection standards for exterior elements including the driveway call for the inspector to observe these elements with respect to their effect on the condition of the building (for example, evaluating if the driveway contributes to water penetration in the home). The inspector, however, shouldn't overlook the condition of the element itself.

The driveway should be level and there should be no heaving in sections. It should slope away from the home or garage. Sometimes this is not possible, depending on the house lot. In this case it is recommended that a drain be installed/located at the base of the driveway to reduce the chance of water penetration into the house/garage structure.

Asphalt

Asphalt is the most common driveway material.

Watch for large cracks or potholes. These can cause vehicle damage, and can also pose a tripping hazard.

Maintenance will include sealing every few years or as needed. Sealing will reduce water-related deterioration.

Concrete

Again, major cracks or other damage can be cause for concern. Fortunately, concrete driveways require no real maintenance other than sealing cracks. However, concrete will show discoloration—such as from oil stains—more easily.

- Add concrete walkway/driveway: $3.50 to $8.00/square foot
- Install asphalt driveway: $5 to $12/square yard
- Resurface asphalt driveway: $4 to $6/square yard

Patios and Decks

Patios are often constructed of materials similar to those used in driveways and walkways, but may also be made of other products such as slate or flagstone. After evaluating the patio's general condition, your primary concern should be the slope. It should slope away from the house to allow for water runoff and drainage.

Decks are generally subject to constant exposure to the elements, so the most common problems are rotting and splitting.

Rotting is a common problem with decks.

Pay careful attention to the condition of supporting posts—they should be free of rot, decay, or other damage and must be adequately sized for the deck (see the following figure). Synthetic decks—available at home improvements stores—are designed to be low-maintenance and less prone to rotting and other problems.

Check the condition of supporting posts.

 Nuts and Bolts _____

> Some materials, such as redwood and cedar, are great for deck construction because they're more resistant to rot. Using preservatives on wood may prolong its life. Decks and wood patios in contact with the ground are more prone to decay.

The next important component of deck construction would be the fasteners used to connect the various elements of the deck. Typically nails are used, although screws are becoming more common. Quality fasteners will not rust, which is a common problem. In addition to the quality of the fastener, the type of fastener will have an impact on the service life of a deck. Properly constructed decks should have *lag bolts* used at primary connections, such as to the house, and joist hangers should be used where connected to the beams. Nails should never be used to connect a deck to a building.

House Keys _____

A **lag bolt** is a large, hex-head bolt or screw which solidly attaches wood framing components.

Flashings between the deck and house are critical. Railings will be required per local building code. The requirements are based upon the vertical distance above ground level. Additionally, there will be specific requirements related to the height of the railing and space between the openings of the vertical railing members. Deck stairs also require railings or guards on both sides if there are more than two risers (see the following figure).

The last aspect of deck inspection is to check the support footing and bracing of the deck. Very high decks require additional bracing.

Deck-related expenses:

- Complete deck addition (average size, treated): $4,000 to $10,000
- Repair existing deck: $10 to $25/square foot

© HouseMaster

Keep an eye on the deck frame for signs of trouble.

Porches

A porch is typically an open or semi-open elevated structure, protected by a roof and designed for the support of furniture and people. Construction can be of a variety of materials including concrete, masonry, wood, and metal. Vertical support should be provided at all corners, either by connection to the house or by support posts or piers. See the photo that follows for an example of settling, a common problem with porches.

© HouseMaster

Settling is a common problem with porches.

Watch out for any signs of sinking, buckling, or warping involving your porch. The porch should not appear to be pulling away from the home.

A wooden porch should have some kind of sturdy foundation, so as to prevent it resting directly on soil, as this would cause moisture to rot the porch floor.

Porch columns or supports should be sturdy and in good repair. If the porch floor is exposed to the elements, it should slope away from the home.

Railings should be secure and in good condition.

Porch expenses:

- Add glassed-in porch: $8,000 to $12,000
- Add screened-in porch: $3,000 to $5,000

Balconies

A balcony is typically an open exterior structure designed for support of light furniture and people, and it is supported by the house structure itself, without the benefit of posts supported by footings. Balconies vary greatly by style, size, and design, but usually cost at least several hundred dollars and can run into the thousands.

Balconies with a *cantilever* design are often the most problematic.

Balconies are a popular residential feature, especially in warmer climates.

Because a cantilevered balcony is part of the house itself, conditions may be present that affect the house structure. A properly constructed balcony should be pitched away from the house to allow water to drain away from the house structure.

The largest concern is deterioration of the cantilevered beams, which are an extension of the house
floor joists. Since floor joists are typically untreated
lumber, the extension that protrudes into the exterior
environment is subject to the elements and deterioration. The second major concern is the area where
the joists exit the house. This area, no matter how
well protected, is subject to water intrusion.

House Keys

If a construction element is **cantilevered**,
it extends beyond the boundaries of its
supports. In the case of a balcony, cantilevered design means that it is supported
only at one end where it attaches to the
home.

Steps

With wooden steps, check for warping, buckling, or
splintering. Watch cement steps for cracks. Steps
should have a handrail that is sturdy and in good
condition.

Steps should be level, with risers evenly spaced.

Expenses:

- Rebuild masonry steps: $700 to $1200
- Replace wood steps: $20 to $40/foot

The Least You Need to Know

- Pay special attention to attached garages, to keep your home and family safe.
- Decks and porches must be protected and monitored for weather-related damage.
- Cantilevered balconies pose specific safety and structural concerns.

Fireplaces and Chimneys

In This Chapter

- Should you care about creosote?
- The importance of chimney liners
- Your chimney needs a rain cap

Fireplaces are a common feature in many homes today, although they generally don't serve as the main heating sources in newer homes as they did years ago. Fireplaces can be romantic, and are a nice way to make your living room cozy on a cold winter night. But they have special maintenance and safety concerns that you must pay attention to.

Traditional Fireplaces

Traditionally, fireplaces were made of masonry, with a brick or stone facing and hearth, and a brick-lined chamber. These types of fireplaces needed to be supported on a sturdy foundation because they were very heavy. A traditional brick or stone fireplace can be a work of art that adds a special unique touch to a home.

Gas-Burning Fireplaces

Gas units have been available for many years for use in masonry and metal fireplaces. These devices are popular because they eliminate the smoke and hassle of burning wood. As with any fuel-burning device, however, proper venting is needed to prevent the buildup of potentially harmful gases. New "ventless" units, designed to burn efficiently and with sensors to monitor the amount of combustion air present, are now approved for use in many areas. These units do not require venting systems that add to the cost or restrict the placement of the unit. While the new ventless units burn efficiently and technically do not require vents, they can still contribute to indoor air pollution concerns. In addition, since water is a by-product of combustion, regular use can add significant amounts of potentially damaging moisture inside the house. Check these units frequently for any signs of damage.

Older gas units often burn inefficiently and produce substantial amounts of potentially harmful gases, including carbon monoxide. As a safety precaution, many manufacturers and codes require that any damper in the venting system be permanently fixed in an open position.

Firebox/Smoke Chamber

Check the condition of mortar work, bricks, and grouting. Make sure that there are adequate clearances from combustible materials.

Push on the firebricks in the rear wall of the firebox. If the bricks are loose or the mortar in the joints has deteriorated, then the firebricks need to be reset or the joints need to be regrouted. If you can do this yourself, you could save yourself hundreds of dollars.

Signs of Trouble

Watch for smoke staining or other signs of improper or inadequate venting. Any obvious blockage of the flue would also be a problem. Rust or water stains are often caused by water seepage. This means that you probably either don't have a rain cap or that your flue may be misaligned.

Creosote Buildup

If you notice a heavy creosote buildup, that's a sign that your air ventilation is inadequate, and it isn't allowing the fire to burn hot enough. Creosote looks like soot, and over time it starts to look like a glaze or glassy coating. An oversized flue will allow for the combustion gases to cool before they vent, thereby depositing creosote onto the flue liner. Too small of a flue will not allow enough of the combustion gases to escape and you may have a backup of gases into the house.

Blockages

Blockages in fireplaces will be evident by smoke odors in the room and smoke stains on the fireplace brickface or mantle. Corrosion in metal fireplaces or on metal dampers in masonry or metal fireplaces is an indication of water getting in, possibly because the chimney needs a rain cap.

Leaks

Chimney leaks are a fairly common home-maintenance problem. Check the flashing around the chimney. You should have L-shaped flashing under every row of shingles, with a second flashing in the mortar joints. If you only have one piece of flashing connecting the roof to the brick, it can shift or pull loose.

Other Points of Interest

Other specific items to look for on masonry chimneys include signs of movement or a gap at the point where the chimney meets the house. Pay attention to the flashings between the chimney and the house, and to the condition of the cap and exposed flue liners.

Flue Liners

A flue liner in a masonry chimney can be made of clay, ceramic, or metal conduit. They are intended to direct combustion products to the outside atmosphere and to protect the chimney walls from heat and corrosion.

Chimney liners serve three main functions:

- They protect the house from heat transfer to combustible materials.

- They protect the masonry from corrosive byproducts of combustion.

- They provide a correctly sized flue for the optimum efficiency of the appliance attached to it. Incorrectly sized flues can lead to poor drafting, excessive creosote buildup, and the production of carbon monoxide with conventional fuels.

The Chimney Cap

A rain cap (to keep water, animals, and birds out) should cover your chimney. This will help prevent corrosion on the *damper* and other metal chimney parts.

House Keys

A **damper** is a valve that regulates the flow of air inside the flue of a furnace or fireplace. A flue is a closed-in section in a fireplace that directs flames, smoke, and gases outside. The hearth is the fireproof surface of a fireplace.

Hearth

The hearth is the brick or stone floor of a fireplace. The hearth should extend beyond the front opening of the fireplace into the room. This gives protection from logs or embers that may fall out into the room.

The Bottom Line on Chimneys

Here are some typical chimney-related expenses:

- Flue cleaning: $100 to $150
- Replace damper in existing opening: $175 to $300
- New fireplace with two-story chimney: $8,000 to $15,000
- Repair chimney cap: $100 to $200 each

The Least You Need to Know

- Watch for signs of chimney corrosion, deterioration, or creosote buildup.
- A chimney cap is important in keeping moisture, animals, and birds out of your chimney.
- Be sure that your flue liner is the correct size for your chimney.

Chapter 12

Siding, Insulation, and Gutters

In This Chapter

- Aluminum vs. vinyl siding
- Insulation saves you big bucks
- The importance of R-value

Siding, insulation, and gutters all have somewhat similar purposes. They all protect your home from elements, and help to prevent water damage. Often overlooked or taken for granted, these three home features can really save you lots of time and money in home repairs.

Your Siding System

The exterior *cladding* on the walls of a house (sheathing, barriers, siding, trim, and finishes) should be considered a system. If all components are not compatible and installed properly, it will not function as intended, which is to provide a reasonably water-resistant covering for the house. The type of siding and trim used will also greatly affect the appearance of the house and long-term cost of maintenance.

House Keys

Cladding is the exterior covering of the structural members of a building.

The most common types of siding materials are true wood products, wood-based composites (hardboard, plywood, etc.), cement and masonry products (stucco, brick, stone, and concrete block), Exterior Insulation and Finish Systems (EIFS), and metal products.

The locale, climate, and type of construction play a major role in determining the type of siding materials. Until the mid-1900s, wood and masonry were the most common. Since the 1970s, there has been a drastic increase in the variety of siding products available.

Aluminum and Vinyl Siding

Siding made from aluminum and vinyl is a very popular home-exterior material, due in large part to its almost maintenance-free nature and its availability in a wide range of colors and styles.

See the photo that follows for an example of residential siding.

Siding is a popular exterior residential material.

The most common problem with aluminum siding is its tendency to fade over time (see the following photo). It also dents fairly easily. Vinyl doesn't fade or dent as easily, but it contracts and expands more than aluminum siding. So vinyl siding tends to crack more, especially in colder climates.

© HouseMaster

Aluminum siding is also a popular material.

Wood Siding

Wood siding is available in shingles, shakes, panels, and boards (see the photo that follows). Many homeowners like the "natural" look of wood shingles— but this material is especially vulnerable to damage from insects and moisture.

Watch for buckling, splitting, and cracking.

© HouseMaster

Wood siding is more common on older homes.

Hardboard Siding

Hardboard siding (also known as composition board siding) is a composite wood product that is among the least expensive of the siding products. However, it has an increased tendency to swell. Watch for signs of moisture penetration and cracking or rotting.

 Home Alarms

There was a large class-action suit involving several manufacturers who were accused of producing defective siding. Homeowners should find out whether the maker of their hardboard siding was involved in this class-action suit.

Common Problems: Siding

The most common cladding-system defects include water infiltration and decay of wood or wood-based products.

Other common siding problems include dents, fading, cracks, and buckling.

If you have a small section of siding that is dented or damaged, it's usually possible just to replace that section. However, it can be tricky to get the siding lined up correctly, and it's sometimes difficult to get new siding that matches the exact shade of the old siding.

Putting up siding can be challenging, and since many siding problems can be traced to improper installation, this is probably a job best left to a professional.

The Bottom Line on Siding

Siding expenses:

- Siding repair: $5 to $10/square foot
- Paint siding: $.70 to $.90/square foot
- Complete house re-siding (average): $5,000 to $7,000

Insulation

Insulation can be worth its weight in gold. A well-insulated home is much more economical and energy-efficient (not to mention a lot less drafty) than a home that isn't properly insulated. It's shocking how much money you'll spend in heating and cooling if your home isn't adequately insulated. In fact, in a poorly insulated home, up to a third of your heating and energy costs will literally be going right through the roof.

Your home should have insulation in the walls and ceilings, and, ideally, in the basement, crawl space, and anywhere else where heat might escape.

Moisture reduces insulation's effectiveness, so it's important to keep it dry. See the photo that follows for an example of moisture staining.

© HouseMaster

Watch out for moisture staining on sheathing.

Often, a barrier will be placed on top of the insulation to help prevent water penetration (see the photo that follows). This is known as a *vapor retarder*.

House Keys

A **vapor retarder** is a layer of material that serves as a barrier to keep moisture from penetrating insulation. Insulation with an attached vapor retarder is called faced insulation, while insulation without a vapor retarder is called unfaced insulation.

Insulation between rafters.

Installing Insulation

Fiberglass insulation is notoriously itchy and irritating to the skin, and can also be harmful when inhaled. This is one of the main reasons why most homeowners don't try to install insulation themselves. However, some manufacturers have come out with modern insulation products that are more do-it-yourselfer friendly. For example, Owens Corning touts its Miraflex insulation (which is covered in a polyethylene wrap) as being virtually itch free and much easier to handle and install than traditional insulation products. See the photos that follow for an example of a home that lacks proper insulation and insulation at soffits.

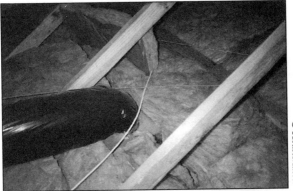

© HouseMaster

It's important to make sure your home is properly insulated.

© HouseMaster

Insulation at soffits.

R-Value

Insulation is primarily used to reduce the rate of heat transfer from areas of high temperature to those of lower temperature. The ability of a material to slow this movement of heat is referred to as its R-value. The higher the R-value, the longer it takes heat to move through the material. See the photo for an example of an R-value label.

© HouseMaster

For best results, make sure insulation has an adequate R-value.

Something to Dwell On

In addition to increasing thermal resistance in a house, insulation also increases occupant comfort, reduces sound transmission, reduces the size of heating and cooling equipment required, and minimizes energy costs.

Here are some general guidelines as to the R-value (per inch) of common insulation materials:

- Fiberglass: 1.7 to 3.6
- Rock wool blanket: 3.1 to 3.7
- Extruded polystyrene: 4.0 to 5.3

The R-value of a layered material can be found by adding the R-values of each layer. In other words, if you have a layer of 3.6 R-value fiberglass insulation 5 inches thick, the total R-value will be 18.

Signs of Trouble with Insulation

Watch for mold, dampness, or other signs of water penetration. Unfortunately, once insulation has been subject to water damage, you'll usually have to just get rid of it and replace it with new insulation.

 Home Alarms

Vapor barriers should be positioned on the warm side of any insulated components between the conditioned and unconditioned spaces. Only one vapor barrier should be installed. A second layer (plastic) above or adjacent to another layer may trap moisture and cause consequential damage. Also, insulation should not block ventilation provisions. Adequate ventilation should be provided to prevent excessive heat and moisture buildup.

You should also, of course, make sure that you *have* insulation (when co-author Bobbi bought her

100-year-old house, the insulation consisted of wads of cloth and paper stuffed into the walls) and that the insulation is adequate.

The amount of insulation required varies with the location in the structure and the area of the country. R-19 is the absolute minimum in ceilings in any area; however, this may go up to a requirement of R-38 in colder climates. Exterior walls are typically a minimum of R-11, going up to R-19. R-19 is also typical in a crawl space.

The Bottom Line on Insulation

Here's what you can expect to pay for insulation projects:

- Install vapor barrier: $.15 to $.40/square foot
- Add 6 inches of fiberglass insulation in attic floor: $.75 to $1.50/square foot
- Add blown-in insulation: $1 to $2/square foot

Brick and Stone Exteriors

Brick is generally considered to be among the strongest and most durable of residential building materials.

Brick and other masonry materials are much heavier than siding and other exterior choices. As a result, a brick home puts a much bigger strain on the foundation. Watch for cracks in the foundation walls or any other signs of strain.

Generally, most bricks used in home construction today are actually what are known as "face bricks." Basically, these are bricks that are used as the façade of a wood frame building. The brick is attached to the frame walls using ties that are generally made of galvanized steel.

The most common problems are cracked, loose, or missing bricks. The good news is, a small section of damaged brickwork can usually be repaired or replaced pretty easily. But masonry can be a time-consuming project, and attention to detail is important because a poorly set layer of brick can be pretty noticeable (especially when contrasted against properly set existing brickwork). So you should probably consider hiring a mason, especially if you need extensive work done or if you have concerns about the structural integrity of the wall or other brick structure.

Stonework is generally more intricate and may be more difficult to repair or replace. Stone also tends to be more expensive and tougher to set properly than brick, so it's probably a good idea to let a mason handle your stonework, to avoid the costly trial-and-error you might incur yourself.

EIFS

Exterior Insulation and Finish Systems (EIFS) are multi-layered exterior wall systems that have been used in home construction since the 1980s (see the photo that follows). A foam insulation board is attached to the wall sheathing, and then a reinforced base coating—which serves as a moisture barrier—is applied directly over the insulation board. The final finish is a stucco-textured coating, which is often called "synthetic stucco."

A special concern with EIFS is the possibility of structural damage, particularly in areas around doors and windows. This is mainly caused by improperly sealed joints where the siding meets the trim. EIFS has a tendency to trap any water that penetrates its surface—creating the perfect setting for rotting and decaying of all nearby wood components.

An example of EIFS.

Gutters

Despite their negative connotation, gutters can be your good friends. It's easy to underestimate how important a good gutter system is—that is, until you're faced with big repair bills for a roof and foundation that have been the victims of water damage. See the photos that follow for a couple examples of common gutter problems.

With old gutters, leaks at the galvanized seams are common.

Another leaking gutter.

Watch out for gutters that are rusted, damaged, or aren't securely attached. Gutters should be clear of debris or blockages. Look for any missing sections or gaps. Also, make sure that joints and corners are sealed and show no signs of leaks or cracks. Perhaps most importantly, gutters should be correctly adjusted and positioned. A gutter does more harm than good if it deposits water directly on the foundation wall, rather than directing water toward a drain or other outlet.

Typical gutter costs:

- New aluminum gutters: $3.75 to $5.50/foot
- Add downspouts: $3 to $4.50/foot

The Least You Need to Know

- Investing in insulation now can save you lots of money later.
- If you want to add a brick or stone exterior, make sure your foundation can handle the weight.
- Gutters are valuable tools in preventing costly water damage.

Structural Framing System

In This Chapter

- The pros and cons of truss framing
- The hazard of balloon framing
- Playing detective to spot problems

The floor framing in a wood frame house consists specifically of the posts, beams, sill pallets, joists, and subfloor. When these components are assembled properly on a foundation (perimeter walls and interior piers) they form a level anchored platform for the rest of the house. In conjunction with the floor framing, you will have wall framing. Wall framing consists of vertical studs and horizontal members (window and door headers, etc.) of exterior and interior walls that support ceilings, upper floors, and the roof.

Framing Construction Methods

Two general types of framing are commonly used: platform construction and balloon-frame construction. The platform method is used more often because of its simplicity. Balloon framing is generally found where stucco or masonry is used on older homes.

Most attics in newer homes today are built using either conventional framing or engineered "truss" framing. With conventional framing (also known as "stick framing"), the roof frame is constructed on-site from several pieces—mainly *beams*, *rafters*, *joists*, and wall *studs*. See the photos that follow for examples of beam problems.

> **House Keys**
>
> A **beam** is a horizontal structural component—usually wood or steel—that supports a heavy load. A **rafter** is the main beam supporting a roof system or a sloping roof framing member. A **joist** is a load-bearing beam that supports floors, roofs, and ceilings. A **stud** is a vertical component—generally wood or metal—which may or may not be load-bearing.

Platform Framing

The wall framing in platform construction is erected above the subfloor and will only extend up to the ceiling of the first floor. The second floor is then built on top of the first floor "platform."

© HouseMaster

Problems with the beams can spell major trouble.

© HouseMaster

An example of beam-timber sag.

Balloon Framing

Balloon framing is a style of construction that is mainly found in old homes. In balloon framing, the exterior wall studs extend from the sill of the first floor (foundation) to the top plate or rafters of the second floor. Balloon framing is generally considered a safety hazard, in that a basement fire could zoom right up through the home's walls pretty much unencumbered.

Truss Construction

A truss is an engineered structure of framing pieces that is pre-assembled off-site. First used in roof construction, trusses are now also frequently found in the floor systems of newer homes. Truss construction is popular with homeowners and many contractors because it speeds up the framing process and can lower construction costs.

Truss construction is considered very reliable, as long as the trusses aren't altered from their engineered design. Watch for any signs that the trusses have been cut or otherwise modified—to accommodate vents or ductwork, for example—as this can weaken the truss.

 Home Alarms _____

Trusses aren't designed to support your family heirlooms and other attic contents. Actually, the beams in conventional framing aren't intended to serve as makeshift shelves, either. You don't want to compromise the effectiveness and safety of your framing system simply to get a little more storage space, so find somewhere else to store your stuff.

Signs of Trouble with Structural Framing

Much of the framing structure of a home is hidden behind walls, under floors, and above ceilings. During a home inspection, the visible areas of framing—in the attic, basement, etc.—will be checked, with a little detective work added in to round out the evaluation.

Sloping floors and major cracks in the walls or ceilings, doors, and windows that are out of *plumb*—these can all be signs of potential structural problems. Then again, these "red flags" can also have other causes, which is why it's important to have a structural engineer or other expert investigate.

 House Keys _____

Plumb means precisely vertical— perfectly straight up and down.

Also watch out for joists that are resting on interior dividers or other components not designed to bear considerable weight.

With roof framing, watch out for sloped roofs that are sagging noticeably. Inadequate bracing or rafters may cause this, or the roof may have had several extra layers of material added, thus significantly increasing its weight to a point that is straining the framing.

Watch all wood components for signs of mold or insect damage, including soft wood, tunneling, and damp areas. Fortunately, if caught early enough, these problems can often be treated relatively easily and inexpensively, before costly structural damage occurs.

The Bottom Line on Framing Repairs

Here's what you can expect to pay for some common framing-related repairs:

- Replace main beam: $30 to $75/foot
- Reinforce exposed joists: $10 to $20/foot
- Replace exposed joists: $15 to $25/foot

The Least You Need to Know

- Truss construction makes the building process faster and cheaper than conventional framing.
- Balloon framing is no longer commonly used because it's a fire hazard.
- Sloping floors and major wall cracks can be signs of serious structural framing damage.

Ancillary Inspections

In This Chapter

- A package deal can be a good bargain
- Those terrible termites
- Sidestepping a septic problem

Ancillary services are evaluations that aren't usually included in your basic home inspection. However, they can often be a valuable service and—depending upon the inspection company—you may be able to get a reasonably priced package deal if you have these "extras" done at the same time as your basic inspection.

Some examples of specialized inspection services are termite inspections, radon screenings, checking of pool/spa, landscaping, and checking of detached garages. In this chapter, we will cover some of the "extra" inspection services you might want to have performed.

Mold

Mold is a hot topic that's been all over the news lately. We've probably all seen the horror stories of unsuspecting homeowners forced to abandon their homes (and walk away from the financial investment) due to a serious mold problem.

But behind the media hype is a justifiable reason for concern. Mold has been linked to serious health problems—not to mention water penetration (which is usually the breeding ground for mold) that can cause major structural damage to your home.

Mold is especially likely in damp climates, or in homes that have any kind of leaks or water penetration. If you suspect your home is a candidate for a mold problem, look into getting a mold inspection right away. Unfortunately, the remediation of an extensive mold infestation will likely require significant invasive repair work such as the removal of sheetrock in the house and repairs to damaged framing.

Asbestos

Asbestos—a naturally occurring fiber found in rocks—was a common ingredient in many building and construction products, mainly because of its fire-resistant qualities. It was frequently used to cover pipes or to insulate ductwork. However, asbestos fibers have been shown to cause serious lung damage. Any asbestos in your home should be covered or removed.

Something to Dwell On _____

A good, smart home inspector will not point out asbestos in the home. What a good, smart inspector will do for his or her client is to point out suspected asbestos-containing material in the home, such as old steam-pipe insulation or old floor and ceiling tiles. Conclusive analysis cannot be performed visually without laboratory testing. Asbestos can be found in materials such as spackling compound, glues, mastics (glues used to secure counter tops and floor tiles), composite materials for counter tops, and countless other materials.

Carbon Monoxide (CO)

You can't see it or smell it, but it can kill you. Carbon monoxide is a serious safety concern—it kills or injures thousands of people every year. Common sources of carbon monoxide in the home include furnaces, water heaters, fireplaces, and wood stoves. Attached garages can also pose major risks for a carbon-monoxide problem.

Carbon-monoxide detectors should be a must for every home, but don't be too reliant on them. Many carbon-monoxide detectors don't sound the alarm until CO levels have already reached a dangerous, life-threatening level.

The best way to handle a CO problem is to prevent it from happening in the first place. A home inspector who specializes in CO problems can give you tips on preventing these deadly fumes, and can point out any possible CO sources that already exist in your home.

Underground Fuel Tanks

In many parts of the country, heating oil for boilers and hot water heaters are often stored in underground tanks on the property. These tanks are typically 550 gallons or larger, giving them an advantage over in-house tanks, which typically only hold 275 gallons. For many different reasons—including the quality of the steel (and coatings) used for the tanks, soil characteristics, and age—steel tanks will corrode. When this happens, the tanks will leak. A leaking fuel tank poses a risk to the environment by contaminating the soil and possibly the water table.

 Home Alarms _____

> Most homeowner insurance policies won't cover the cost of treating soil that has become contaminated as a result of a leaking fuel tank. It's important to have these tanks inspected so that you can spot problems while they (and their repair bill) are small.

It's important to have a proper test performed on the tank, as this can be a costly problem. Cleanup costs range from a few thousand dollars to hundreds of thousands (if ground-water contamination occurs). Fuel tanks that test positive for leakage should be properly abandoned or removed according to the local requirements.

Radon

Radon gas is a naturally occurring byproduct of decaying uranium. Radon levels in the outside air we breathe (ambient levels) are very low and not considered a concern. However, exposure to concentrated levels of radon gas has been linked to cancer and other health problems. Radon testing will determine if the radon gas levels in the home have reached dangerous levels.

How much radon gas builds up in a home is dependant on the area you live in (geological conditions under the house) and the type of construction of the home. New, tighter houses have less air exchange and are less drafty than older homes, and therefore can have higher levels. Sump pits, cracks in floors, and dirt crawl-space floors are all potential contributing factors. Radon remediation is quite simple and will probably cost you about $1,200.

Termites and Other Insects

Termites and other wood-destroying insects (WDIs) can cause an incredible amount of damage to your home—meaning hefty repair bills. Also, many lending institutions require a termite inspection before approving a mortgage. Areas of the northwest and wet climates also require wood-destroying organism inspections (WDO), which would include mold and fungus.

When checking for WDI or WDO, an inspector will keep a close eye out for conditions conducive to an infestation (such as wood frame in contact with soil, dampness, etc.), in addition to signs of current infestation such as termite mud tunnels and "frass," which are the sawdust-like evidence that carpenter ants are burrowing through your house framing. The tunnels can be located just about anywhere— in the ceiling, behind walls, on the foundation, etc.

© HouseMaster

Termite tunnels can be a sign of a big problem.

Nuts and Bolts

> Termites love moist climates, but have been found all over the United States, even in the coldest or hottest regions. So don't think that you don't need to be concerned about termites if you live in a colder climate.

Septic/Sewer Systems

A septic system can be very expensive—and inconvenient—to repair or replace, so it's a good idea to keep a close eye out for potential problems. Unfortunately, the average homeowner only becomes aware of a septic problem when it becomes blatantly obvious—as in a horrible smell, toilets not draining, etc.

Some inspection companies offer a simple septic-system check as part of their basic service. This is often referred to as a "dye stress test". Dye tablets are flushed down the toilet and a volume of water is put into the system, usually based upon the number of bedrooms. The test will only tell you if the system backs up, bleeds out onto the lawn, or there are septic odors. Each symptom may indicate a potential concern, but a dye test will not provide the information one needs to make an informed decision.

In many areas of the country, such as New Jersey, a septic failure in most cases will require a system upgrade or replacement (typical cost: $15,000 to $30,000). This is why co-author Mike recommends an "open pit" evaluation. A septic company will come out and locate the septic tank, distribution boxes, and leach field. They will open the tank and d-boxes, examining for condition and signs of failure, and will run water and probe the leach fields for high water levels. Considering the cost of a new septic system, we'd put our money on an "open pit" test vs. a cheap dye job.

Home Alarms

Make sure the inspector is actually qualified to perform the ancillary service you need, and will provide the highest level of service available for the industry. Take, for example, dye tests for septic systems. Anyone can do it as long as he or she has the dye. While it may be acceptable for the mortgage lenders, dye tests give no indication as to the condition of the septic tank, leach fields, and other major components of a septic system. An open pit septic evaluation may cost $250 to $450 in some areas, but the customer will have greater piece of mind that the physical conditions of all the septic components have been visually inspected.

Security Systems

A security system is generally not evaluated as part of a basic home inspection. The company that installed your security system most likely provides a monitoring/inspection service, and they might be your best choice since they'd be the most familiar with your specific system. However, many inspection companies also offer a security-system check as one of their extra services.

The Least You Need to Know

- Make sure that the contractor has the specialized skills necessary to perform an ancillary inspection.
- A wood-destroying insect inspection can reveal termites and other bugs that can cause pricey damage.
- Having your septic system checked can help avoid a costly and messy disaster.
- Plan ahead and save money by getting ancillary services performed at the same time as your basic inspection.

Chapter 15

Finding a Home Inspector

In This Chapter

- Finding someone to do the job
- How to spot a good inspector (and a bad one)
- Insurance, licenses, and other details

"Okay, you convinced me. I want to get a home inspection. But where do I find one of these elusive inspectors?"

Real-estate brokers often refer homebuyers to a home inspector, so you can start by asking your broker. You can also check your local phone book under "Building Inspections" or "Home Inspection."

Inspector Assessment

It's not that tough to find a home inspector—although it does require a little extra effort to make sure you have a *good* home inspector.

> **Something to Dwell On** _____
>
> Of homebuyers polled in a 2001 sur-
> vey, 69 percent of those who ordered
> home inspections found their inspectors
> through recommendations from a real-
> estate agent.

Referrals

In addition to real estate agents, attorneys and
mortgage brokers may also be able to recommend
a good home inspector.

Checking Credentials

The best way to make sure you've got a good,
qualified home inspector is to look for a company
or inspector that belongs to a reputable trade
organization, such as the American Society of
Home Inspectors (ASHI) at www.ashi.com or the
National Institute of Building Inspectors (NIBI) at
www.nibi.com.

If an inspector says he or she is a member of NIBI
or another trade group, don't just take his or her
word for it—call the organization and verify this
info. Of course, you could avoid this problem al-
together if you use the "locate an inspector" link
on the organization's website to find an inspector
in the first place.

Inspectors who belong to a group such as ASHI
must follow that organization's standards of

practice and ethical guidelines. ASHI's professional code of ethics prohibits members from engaging in conflict-of-interest activities that might compromise their objectivity. So an ASHI member inspector cannot, for example, use the inspection to solicit or refer repair work.

 Nuts and Bolts

> One of the best things about the NIBI is the fact that it's a training center, and new inspectors are taken on training inspections. In contrast, some organizations allow inspectors-in-training to hone their skills on unsuspecting customers.

NIBI's code of ethics also prohibits inspections on properties in which the inspector may have an interest or potential interest. In addition, NIBI stresses the importance of professionalism and respect for property.

All trade organizations are not created equal. Within any trade, you have associations and other groups that vary from wonderful to sub-par, and the home-inspection business is no different. A few "trade organizations" for inspectors simply require the payment of a fee in order to become a member. Check out the various trade organizations, and study their membership requirements (as well as their standards of practice and code of ethics) carefully.

If a home inspector belongs to ASHI or another trade organization, the inspector most likely will prominently display the association's logo that one would find in their ads or on their website. So it's pretty easy to find out that info, often without even having to call the inspector.

ASHI is the oldest professional association for independent home inspectors. ASHI Members are required to follow the Society's Code of Ethics and to obtain continuing education credits in order to keep current with the latest in building technology, materials, and professional skills. However, NIBI requires inspectors to carry E&O (errors and omissions) liability insurance, while ASHI does not.

 Nuts and Bolts

> The most commonly accepted standards and inspection guidelines are those issued by the ASHI and the National Institute of Home Inspectors (NAHI). In certain areas, inspectors also meet or exceed standards established by other agencies, such as the Texas Real Estate Commission (TREC), the Canadian Association of Home and Property Inspectors (CAHPI), or the California Real Estate Inspection Association (CREIA).

As we mentioned in Chapter 1, the standards of practice are important because they establish minimum uniform standards that inspectors use as guidelines for evaluating a home. So there's no guesswork involved, and an inspector is not just giving his or her opinion.

The Guarantee

A good home-inspection company will also offer some kind of guarantee, although the exact specifics vary widely. Whatever kind of guarantee your home inspector offers, make sure you completely understand it and get it in writing.

Asking Around

Word-of-mouth is another great way to find a home inspector. Ask friends and relatives—especially those who have bought or sold a home recently—for the names of inspectors they've used and liked.

They may also be able to give you a good idea of how much you can expect to pay, what guarantees (if any) the company offers, and what kind of report you'll receive following the inspection.

Hey, You Got a License for That Clipboard?

Licensing is a nice extra safeguard, but it won't guarantee you get a good inspector. Licensing guidelines can vary widely—many do not require ongoing training, provide any technical assistance, or require malpractice insurance.

Since licensing requirements can vary greatly, don't use that as your only criteria for choosing an inspector. Be sure to take all of the inspector's credentials and experience into account when making your decision.

Ongoing Training

No matter how much experience an inspector has, he or she should still receive ongoing training. Like any other skilled professionals, home inspectors need to keep up with current news, trends, and developments in their industry. Look for an inspection company that requires employees to get a certain amount of ongoing training. It's also a plus if the company tests its inspectors regularly.

Be sure to ask what kind of ongoing training your home inspector receives. An inspection company that doesn't require employees to receive ongoing training may not be conscientious about keeping current with systems and components found in modern homes.

Liability Insurance and Other Coverage

It's extremely important to make sure that your home inspector has insurance, especially Professional Liability Insurance. If an inspector doesn't have this insurance, it could mean that he or she hasn't been in business very long or has a poor track record.

Professional Liability Insurance, also known as Errors and Omissions (E&O) Insurance, is much like malpractice insurance. This gives consumers some recourse should a mistake happen. Be sure to request proof of insurance coverage before the inspection begins.

> **Something to Dwell On**
>
> Don't forget general liability insurance. What if an inspector's flashlight falls over on the kitchen table, breaking the figurine that was just taken off the wedding cake a few days earlier? Did you ever use an electric garage-door opener with the door locked? The metal doors crunch up like a soda can. Someone will be asked to pay. Also, not unheard of, what if a buyer's inspector gets hurt on a property? Will he or she hold the seller accountable because the inspector failed to maintain workers compensation insurance? Co-author Mike assures you that none of these situations are enjoyable, so be sure to double-check that your inspector is fully insured.

The Inspection Report

The inspection report is another important factor to consider when choosing an inspector. Some inspectors provide highly detailed reports, while others give you something very general and vague.

While a fancy-looking report is nice, don't overestimate the presentation at the expense of substance. Computer-generated narrative reports may be neater, easier to read, and impressive, but also may be filled with so much boilerplate and disclaimer information that the true sense is lost in the reporting. And remember, the report is only as good as the inspector writing it. The most qualified inspector may not necessarily be the one with the pricey computer in his or her truck. Then again, handwritten reports may be more to the point but lacking in detail, sloppy, and hard to read.

 Home Alarms _____

> Many home-inspection firms simply provide a cursory report that classifies an element simply as "functioning" or "not functioning." This really isn't very helpful—as a system can be functional but in poor condition, or can be functional and expected to still have a long life span.

When it comes to inspection reports, there is no "perfect" kind. It's not a one-size-fits-all thing, because different customers have different preferences. Co-author Mike has noticed that different personality types like different report formats. By his observation, attorneys like typewritten reports, blue-collar guys like down-and-dirty handwritten check lists, and nerds like gadgets and computer reports.

Here are some questions to ask about the inspection report:

- Can I see a sample report?
- When will the report be available?
- How detailed and specific is the report?

State Laws

A few states have passed legislation governing home inspectors. This serves as an added safeguard, so that consumers in those states can have some extra reassurance that they'll be dealing with a qualified inspector. Most home-inspection laws dictate the minimum insurance coverage an inspector must have, the specific standards of practice that must be followed, and educational or experience requirements.

Something to Dwell On

In Arkansas, all home inspectors must register with the Secretary of State, have at least $100,000 in general liability insurance, and can't perform repairs on a building that he or she has inspected in the past year. Illinois, meanwhile, requires inspectors to take a state-approved examination. For details on regional laws in your area, contact your state officials' office or check out ASHI's website at www.ashi.com.

Sure Signs of a Bad Inspector

When it comes to home inspectors, there are a few obvious "red flags" that should send you running in the other direction:

- The inspector completes the entire inspection in less than 10 minutes.

- The inspector offers to give you "a good deal" on home repairs, or tells you that his or her cousin can fix that crack in your driveway.

- The inspector writes the inspection report in crayon on the back of a pizza box.

- The inspector doesn't see the need for insurance, since he thinks that he does a "pretty good job."

Final Thoughts and Resources

We hope we've made the home-inspection process a little clearer and less intimidating for you. By taking you step by step through the process, and showing you how to find a qualified inspector, we think we've greatly improved your chances of having a positive home-inspection encounter. While we can't guarantee your home will get a glowing inspection report, we're pretty confident that the inspection process will be an educational, enlightening, and hopefully enjoyable experience.

Here are some other resources if you want to do some "further inspection" on your own:

- American Society of Home Inspectors: www.ashi.com
- Canadian Association of Home and Property Inspectors: www.cahpi.ca
- HouseMaster: www.housemaster.com
- National Association of Certified Home Inspectors: www.nachi.org
- National Association of Home Inspectors: www.nahi.org
- National Institute of Building Inspectors: www.nibi.com

The Least You Need to Know

- Carefully check the inspector's credentials, reputation, and insurance coverage.
- If you want a detailed written report, check in advance to make sure the inspection service provides one.
- Ask about a guarantee, and get it in writing.
- Consider whether an extra, specialized inspection service might be a good deal for you.
- Investigate any state or local laws governing home inspections.
- Watch out for referrals to contractors and other sure signs of a bad inspector.

Glossary

agreement of sale   A contract between the buyer and seller involving the purchase of a home.

annual fuel utilization efficiency (AFUE)
Measures a furnace or boiler's efficiency.

backdrafting   When fumes escape into the home instead of venting to the exterior.

backfill   Earth installed in the area excavated for the construction of the foundation walls.

cantilevered   Extends beyond the boundaries of its supports.

circuit breakers   Switches inside the electrical panel that will stop power to a certain area of the home in the event of a power overload.

component   Smaller part of a system.

compressor   Circulates coolant through the air conditioning unit.

double-hung window   Opens from both the top and bottom.

drip loop   A loop in the service conductor that minimizes the chance of water penetration.

eaves   The horizontal, lower edge of a sloped roof.

evaporator coil   Absorbs heat from the air prior to it entering the cooled space.

faced insulation   Insulation with an attached vapor retarder (kraft paper or foil-backed paper).

flashing   A barrier that seals the joint(s) when a roof plane is interrupted.

footer (or footing)   The concrete base that the foundation sits on.

foundation   A wall, usually made from some form of masonry material, on which the house's framing is built. The foundation provides structural support and is one of the most critical parts of a home or building.

further evaluation   Examination and analysis by a qualified professional or service technician beyond that provided by the home inspection.

fuse   An electrical overload protection device that will blow out if an overload occurs.

ground fault circuit interrupters (GFCIs)
Outlets that provide extra protection against electrical shock in case of a short circuit.

home inspection   Process by which an inspector visually examines the readily accessible systems and components of a home, and evaluates those components according to established standards.

joist   Parallel beam set from wall to wall to support the floor or ceiling.

junction box   A small box containing spliced or connected wiring and cables.

knob-and-tube wiring   An old type of wiring that is not grounded.

main panel   The central distribution point for the electrical circuits that run to lights, receptacles, and appliances throughout the house.

metal insulation supports   Wire rods or crisscrossed wire used to hold floor insulation in place.

pane   The actual piece of glass in a window.

pitch   The degree of roof incline expressed as the ratio of the rise to the span.

retaining wall   A boundary, usually several feet high and commonly made of stone, designed to keep water or soil from encroaching on a property.

rise   The vertical distance from the eaves line to the ridge.

run   The horizontal distance from the eaves to a point directly under the ridge. Equals one half the span.

sash   The portion of the window that slides or turns when the window is opened and closed.

service drop   The lines running from the utility pole to the house.

sheathing   The outer skin of the framing to which siding is installed.

shower pan   The bottom-most part of the shower assembly.

shower stall   An enclosed unit that contains only a shower (as opposed to combination shower/tub units).

slope   The degree of roof incline expressed as the ratio of the rise to the run.

soffit   The finished underside of the eaves.

span   The horizontal distance from eaves to eaves.

standards of practice   Minimum, uniform standards for home inspections, established by organizations such as the American Society of Home Inspectors or industry publications.

subfloor   The structural material that spans across floor joists.

system   Combination of interacting or interdependent components, assembled to carry out one or more functions.

water hammer   The buildup of pressure in the water lines that causes noisy, banging pipes.

weatherhead   A small cap attached to the building to keep the service entrance protected from the elements.

Index